Cognitive Psychology
with a Frame of Reference

Cognitive Psychology with a Frame of Reference

J. P. Guilford
Professor Emeritus of Psychology
University of Southern California

EdITS publishers
SAN DIEGO, CALIFORNIA 92107

First Printing, January, 1979

ISBN: 0-912736-22-4

Library of Congress catalog card number: 78-74137

CONTENTS

Preface   vii

Introduction   ix

PART I: GENERAL PSYCHOLOGICAL THEORY   1

Factorial Angles to Psychology   3

Intelligence Has Three Facets   16 ˙

Executive Functions and a Model of Behavior   26

A Psychology with Act Content, and Form   35

PART II: LEARNING AND MEMORY   47

An Emerging View in Learning Theory   49 ˙

Roles of Intellectual Abilities in the Learning of Concepts   61

Transformation of Information in Learning   68

Varieties of Memory and Their Implications   76

PART III: THE HIGHER MENTAL PROCESSES   93

Basic Conceptual Problems in the Psychology of Thinking   95

More on Creative Thinking and Problem Solving   111

Intellectual Aspects of Decision Making   120

PART IV: SOME EXTENSIONS   133

Intellectual Controls   134
Some Further Considerations   142

APPENDIX: Code to Structure of Intellect Trigrams   157

REFERENCES   158

Preface

This volume is designed to help establish some needed general guidelines for basic, cognitive psychology. In his 1957 presidential address to the American Psychological Association, Lee J. Cronbach decried the lack of communication between what he called "experimental" and "correlational" streams of psychology. This volume should serve to improve this communication by showing that the multivariate experimental approach through factor-analytic investigations of individual differences can be a unique and fruitful source of systematic, taxonomic concepts.

The major system of concepts proposed stems from the Structure-of-Intellect (SI) model, which is described in Chapter 2. This model's general emphasis is on the individual's processing of different kinds of information in various ways—in different codes and forms—which immediately gives it a link with cognitive psychology. References are made to the shortcomings of historical psychological systems, and it is also shown how certain systematic concepts of each general theory were in the direction of various aspects of the SI model.

Special attention is given to problems of learning and memory. A new, broader conception of learning is proposed, and particular attention is given to the learning of concepts and to the roles of transformations and reinforcement in learning. Numerous implications are pointed out for the more usual bivariate experimental investigation of these problems.

The SI model is particularly suited to making contributions toward logical clarifications in the more amorphous areas of the "higher mental processes." The very ambiguous concepts regarding thinking, reasoning, problem solving, creative thinking, and decision making can be replaced with SI concepts, which are empirically rooted in that they refer to specific kinds of mental tasks.

Certain features of the SI model can be applied to phenomena of motivation and to voluntary control of behavior, in the form of "executive functions," in both intellectual and motor areas. Multivariate procedures also offer promise for bringing out taxonomic concepts in the areas of feelings and emotions.

Most of the chapters in this volume were reproduced or were extracted from some of my previously published papers, with such editing and revising as were needed in order to avoid some undesirable redundancies, to eliminate some inconsistencies, or occasionally to update views. It was not desirable to eliminate all redundancies, for each previously published essay still has some need to stand by itself. Nor could all inconsistencies be eliminated, since some are embedded in history. The views are essentially consistent, when seen in terms of timing of the publications. Positively speaking, repetitions have the value of providing emphasis and of contributing to a picture of the development of ideas. A few footnotes have been appended in places in order to add information or to update it.

I am very much indebted to the publishers who have granted permissions to reproduce material from the various sources, to my coauthors of some of the articles, and to my wife Ruth for assistance in preparing the manuscript.

J. P. Guilford

Introduction

As the wheels of psychological history turn, there is obviously grow-ing evidence that the behavioristic surge, which started with John Watson in the twenties and reached its peak with Clark Hull in the forties, is definitely on the wane, and that "mentalistic" psychology is staging a robust comeback. Psychology's original aim, to understand mental events, is again a major source of motivation.

Behaviorism's efforts to account for all behavior solely in terms of stimulus-response sequences have definitely made their con-tributions, but this approach has been able to go only a limited distance. It is becoming more generally recognized that organisms actually create their own effective stimuli. There are just too many problems concerning what happens between environmental energies and behavioral responses—problems that will not go away. Although a few behaviorists have made attempts to describe what goes on between stimulus and response, such efforts have failed badly. One result has been the development of a "cognitive" psychology, which is aimed at the understanding of how organisms construct and use their own representations of their environments and of themselves. It is to these representations that organisms react, and in fully understand-ing behavior, we need to come to know them.

In a sense, this trend brings us back to psychology as the erstwhile science of consciousness, but with a very significant difference. The trick has been in the substitution of the concept of "information" for that of "consciousness." Information is, indeed, a much more man-ageable concept, which makes possible a completely objective psychology. This change was no doubt largely instigated by the development of the modern electronic computer. A computer model has some great advantages over traditional models of the telegraph and the telephone, which for years furnished the background conceptions of nervous functions by their similarity to the reflex arc.

For a definition of "cognitive psychology" we can probably do no better than to quote Neisser (1967), who has given broad attention to the subject. He states that cognitive psychology studies "the flow of information in the organism," a conception that he attributes to Broadbent (1963). In neither of these two sources does the author take pains to define "information." Broadbent regards the flow of information as the needed link between behavior and physiological events, and he has invented flow charts on the order of designs for computer programs in order to describe what happens (Broadbent, 1958). The present writer has defined psychological information as "that which the organism discriminates," in recognition of the conception proposed by communication engineers (Guilford, 1967). This statement, however, more accurately applies to "transmitted information."

Brains and Computers

The recognition of the applicability of the concept of information has led some psychologists, such as Garner (1962), to follow communication engineers further by applying the latter's "bit" index of measurement to psychological events. Taking the computer analogy very seriously, some others—E. B. Hunt (1975), for example—have engaged in computer-simulation research and have applied computer-type models very extensively to what is called "artificial intelligence." Newel, Shaw, and Simon (1958) have followed the same route on a smaller scale.

Others have been less enthusiastic about taking this direction. For example, Neisser (1967) suggests that little is gained by applying the bit measure and that the so-called artificial-intelligence programs are "simpleminded, undistractable, and unemotional"—in other words, far from realistic as pictures of human behavior. Other authors—Arib (1970), for example—have pointed out some critical differences between human and computer operations. Among these differences is the fact that the computer solves a problem that is handed to it, whereas man must recognize that a problem exists and must structure it for himself. The computer has to deal with only one problem at a time, but man often faces several problems. Programs for solving problems are also handed to the computer, and they are debugged, while man must construct his own programs, which are probably not debugged. The computer is given a restricted amount of information related to the problem, but enough to solve the problem, while man has additional inputs to contend with and perhaps not all the information he needs for solving the problem. The computer is sure to detect inconsistencies, for it cannot tolerate them, but man overlooks many inconsistencies if they are not sufficiently obvious.

Garvin (1970) believes that computer-simulation research has been done too optimistically. For one thing, it has limited the conception of intelligence to problem solving, and we do not know enough about the psychology of problem solving to provide the knowledge of what is to be simulated. Such research has also failed to deal with the ubiquitous fact of individual differences among problem solvers.

Thus, although the model provided by the computer and its programming has been, and can continue to be, a general demonstration of new fruitful ways of thinking, and also possible analogies to human mental functioning, it does not tell us exactly how the brain operates in its information processing. The basic difference is probably that the computer has no problem of personal survival in a very complex environment. The analogies can indeed be sources of useful hypotheses in psychological research. If nothing else, the computer-simulation effort illustrates the kinds of models of psychological operations that need to be constructed.

Needs for a Frame of Reference
In the days of Wundt, Brentano, and Titchener, there was a great concern regarding system building in psychology. Efforts were directed toward the search for well-defined concepts and meaningful interrelationships among those concepts. Somehow that interest has all but disappeared, at least for mentalistic psychology (Hull did engage in such activity for behaviorism). Perhaps it is the greater range of heterogeneity in modern psychological research, and in the research findings, that discourages current attempts at system construction. One result is that—except for certain concepts that have endured down the ages from faculty psychology, such as perception, memory, and reasoning—most psychological concepts have been in and out depending upon fashions, and little attempt is made to systematize them. There is no well-organized set of concepts, no taxonomy for psychology.

The value of having a taxonomy in a science should be obvious to any member of a scientific group. We need only to note the great value of the chemists' periodic table or the biological models of Linnaeus, the latter as a major basis for Darwin. It is the main thesis of this volume that the Structure-of-Intellect (SI) model can provide a good taxonomy for cognitive psychology. One support for this proposal is the fact that the nature of the model has suggested the definition of intelligence as a systematic set of abilities or functions for processing different kinds of information in various ways. This definition seems to be very much in accordance with that given above for cognitive psychology, and its stress on information is reminiscent of the ancient Romans' identification of intelligence with information.

The empirical evidence for the SI model was derived mainly from the program of the Aptitudes Research Project at the University of Southern California over a twenty-year interval of intensive research. Midway in the program the SI model was constructed and reported (Guilford, 1959b). Full accounts of the model and a summary of the basic research have been subsequently reported (Guilford, 1967, 1977a; Guilford & Hoepfner, 1971). Defense against the most serious criticism may be seen in Chapter 13 of this volume.

A good taxonomy provides both a map and a compass by which one is able to navigate within the realm of one's sphere of interest. It can be the major source of problems to be investigated. It can suggest hypotheses to be tested. It can remind us of the experimental controls that need to be applied. It also provides a background against which results can be interpreted. Finally, it furnishes a common language, hence improves communication. Communicability has been one of the longstanding criteria of scientific validity.

In the course of the chapters that follow, it will be shown how very ambiguous many of the time-honored psychological concepts have been and how they can be replaced with well-defined, empirically based concepts from the SI model. The following chapters will also show how the mental operations go well beyond perception and memory, and will demonstrate that at least thirty kinds of information should be distinguished (only a few are now commonly recognized). It will also be shown how the taxonomy has some uses extending beyond the realm of intelligence and how other kinds of extensions are possible. Applications in the fields of speech, education, and psychotherapy will be touched upon.

Part I
General
Psychological
Theory

The major objective of Chapter 1 is to show that the kinds of variables revealed by experimental application of factor analysis can provide a basis for general psychological theory. From the major concepts thus obtained, such taxonomies as psychology needs can be derived.

From the findings on how individuals differ systematically, factor analysis can lead to information as to how individuals are alike in their psychological functioning. In ordinary behavior, the functional variables and their properties are so interwoven that more customary modes of observation cannot very well isolate the threads of activity. The multivariate approach of factor analysis enables us to do this.

Some of the more familiar theory basic to factor analysis itself is briefly reviewed from a geometric standpoint and traits or dimensions of personality, which have been organized in models of hierarchical or of matrix types, are derived from factorial findings.

Following comments on the history of intelligence testing and of analyses of intellectual abilities, Chapter 2 presents a brief review of the nature of the Structure-of-Intellect (SI) model. Reasons are given for rejecting both Spearman's g and British hierarchical models of intelligence. Hierarchical models imply correlated abilities and oblique factors at several levels of generality. Although I have always rotated factor axes orthogonally, I have never rejected the idea of correlated ability factors. I have simply not trusted oblique rotations as a means for determining those correlations, while believing that orthogonal axes can give satisfactory approximations to psychologically meaningful abilities. If there is to be a hierarchical model for intelligence, the higher-order factors should be along the lines of the SI categories, and the hierarchy would have to be in more than two dimensions.

Chapter 3 introduces the new concept of "executive functions," which are concerned with the mobilization and management of motor responses. As such, they provide operational links between intellectual activity and muscular activity. A resulting model of behavior is presented, incorporating all the major steps between sensory input and motor output in an information-processing system.

Chapter 4 discusses some more general implications of the SI model for psychological theory. It points out how historical systems of psychology have tended to restrict themselves to only certain operational or informational categories of the SI model. In terms of that model, no system was complete. Only the Gestalt psychologists paid much attention to the SI product categories. In this respect, they came closest to the "operational-informational" view derived from the model.

Chapter 1

Factorial Angles To Psychology[1]

Very rarely has it been recognized that factor analysts have anything
to contribute toward the resolution of general systematic issues in
psychology. It must be admitted at the outset that there is as yet no
unified body of psychological theory, as such, that has been developed
from factor-analytic findings. What I shall say on the subject is the
opinion of one person and cannot be represented as an expression for
any group.

The average factor analyst has delayed theory building because
systematic thinking requires information concerning a large number
of psychological factors before the most significant interrelationships
become apparent and systems can take shape.[2] The writer felt no
particular call to consider the relationship of psychological factors to
behavior theory until he faced the problem of presenting in book form
an organized picture of personality from the point of view of factors
(Guilford, 1959a). As for the systematists in psychology who are not
factor analysts, very few have regarded the method of factor analysis
as a scientific tool by which a comprehensive model of the behaving
organism could be derived.[3]

---

[1]Extracted by permission from *Psychological Review,* 1961, 68, 1-20. Originally
based upon a paper presented at the University of Florida, Gainesville, March, 9, 1959,
in a symposium on points of view in psychology.

[2]Earlier steps toward general theory, starting with factors, were made by Spearman
(1923), Burt (1949), Vernon (1950), and Cattell (1957), none of which gained general
acceptance. (Royce, 1973, has more recently made an attempt at a more comprehensive
theory.)

[3]With the exception of Tolman (1932), in his exposition of a theory of purposive
behavior.

Objectives of this Paper

It is the purpose of this paper to show how factor theory and factor-analytic results can provide models and the information upon which a comprehensive theory of behavior could be based. To this end, it will be necessary to present the logical foundation for factor analysis as a scientific method and to see how we can go logically from factors to the kinds of concepts that are more familiar in psychological theory. What can be done at this time [1961] is to indicate some of the implications of the knowledge of factors and their interrelationships for the understanding of the behavior of individuals and some of the more general ideas that follow from these implications. The conclusions have some bearing upon perennial, systematic issues.

Why Factors Have Not Contributed to Psychological Theory

One of the reasons the findings of factor analysis have not contributed more to psychological theory is that many analyses have not been basic studies of the properties of human nature, either by intention or by way of outcome. One practical use of factor analysis is the reduction of correlation data in order to transform them into simpler form. The chances of revealing anything of fundamental psychological interest under these circumstances are rather remote.

Even when the objective is to discover something of general psychological interest, the outcomes are often disappointing. Some analyses of this kind are forced to be mostly exploratory, hence cannot be well planned. An exploratory study can yield suggestions of hypotheses to be further investigated, however. Without good hypotheses there is limitation to the wise choice of experimental variables. The choice of variables to be analyzed together is all important for success. We cannot go into the technical reasons for this statement here, but the well-worn cliché, "you get out of a factor analysis what you put into it" will apply if it is revised to read, "you *cannot* get out of a factor analysis what you *do not* put into it."

Another reason for some failures of factor-analytical studies is the lack of good experimental design. More will be said about this point later, but I should like to warn here that the fact that we have an elaborate computational procedure for treating data does not relieve us of the necessity of observing the ordinary requirements of experimental logic and experimental controls.

Probably one reason that the results of even the better factor analyses are so often rejected as contributions to general psychological knowledge is that the method has been used in the study of individual differences. The fact that these studies have most often been inspired by the interests of vocational psychologists and not by interests in basic problems is relatively incidental. The basic data with which the factor analyst starts are measurements of a large number of individuals in a fairly large number of experimental variables, compared to the much smaller numbers of subjects and variables of the traditional bivariate experimental psychologist. When interpreted psychologically, factors are also conceived as variables on which individuals differ from one another. Psychological theorists, on the other hand, have been interested in how individuals are *alike* and only incidentally in how they *differ*. It is very easy to bridge the gap, but there has been little effort to do so.

In this connection, the factorist could well charge the general theorist with being negligent for not bringing individual differences into the picture when he constructs a system of psychology. No well-known system, with the exception of Tolman's purposive behaviorism, has anything significant to say about individual differences. Individual differences have been recognized as empirical facts, but they have been generally treated as nuisances by the experimental psychologist, and as phenomena of little or no interest by the theorist. The fact that reasonably satisfying systems could be built ignoring individual differences is an important reason for not bringing them into the picture.

One consequence of this general state of affairs is that the theorist who is concerned with personality often finds such systems inadequate for his purposes. Consequently he builds his own theory. But even such a theory often recognizes only implicitly the need for a significant emphasis on individual differences. It rarely does justice to this aspect of the meaning of personality. Such a theorist recognizes that each person is unique, but he does not sufficiently appreciate the fact that it is individual differences that make him unique.

Some Factor Models for Personality

Factor theory has provided the only rigorous models of any consequence that have been proposed to make intelligible the many facets of the phenomena of individual differences. I shall mention three of those models[4] because they are especially relevant to this paper. A multidimensional model is used to represent personality in general, a hierarchical model can represent interrelationships among traits within individuals, and a matrix model can also represent relationships among factors in certain domains of behavior.

A Dimensional Model. The basic model is a multidimensional affair in Euclidian space, each dimension of which represents a unique trait variable. A unique trait can be discovered as a common factor by

---

[4]Other models have been presented by Guttman (1954) and by Lazersfeld (1954).

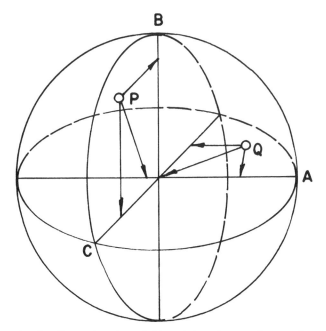

1.1. Example of a dimensional model involving three unique traits, or common factors, A, B, and C, showing characteristic point positions for two individuals, P and Q, with respect to the three personality traits.

analysis. To the extent that an individual's personality can be accounted for in terms of a limited number of common factors, each person can be represented as a point in *n*-dimensional space.

Figure 1.1 illustrates this kind of model, showing only three dimensions, for obvious reasons. Each axis is a linear dimension representing a unique trait along which individuals have characteristic trait positions. Let us say that the axes A, B, and C represent the disparate traits of gregariousness, meticulousness, and emotional stability, with their positive extreme qualities at the labeled ends of the axes. So far as these traits go, person P is described quantitatively by his projections on the three axes. His three projections define a point, which is his characteristic position in this three-dimensional space. The point for P tells us that he is a bit below average in gregariousness, that he is very meticulous, and moderately strong in emotional stability, the average position for each trait being at the origin.

Person Q has another combination of three projections, defining another position in the same space. In *n*-dimensional space, each person has *n* different projections defining a point in that multidimensional space. The fact that he probably changes his position somewhat from time to time need not concern us in this discussion.

Such changes are the reason for the expression "characteristic position" used above. If it is difficult to think of a space with a large number of dimensions, one can think instead of a profile chart, in which the dimensions are laid side by side.

The fact that the axes shown in the figure are orthogonal, or at right angles, is incidental. Actually, factorists generally agree that the best-representing axes often depart from right angles, although they do not agree on how the angular separations shall be determined. Traits at 90-degree separation have no correlation; they are independent. Some degree of correlation is necessary to permit the next type of model to be applied.

A Hierarchical Model. Although the dimensional model just seen provides the basis for the description of individuals, it is better as a representation of variables within populations than as a picture of personality within individuals. One reason is that personality traits are of different degrees of generality, in the sense that some are related to wide ranges of behavior and some to narrower ranges.

A simple example will illustrate. Let us say that Student Z declined an opportunity to cheat while taking a certain examination. This is a specific action; there is no necessary implication concerning Z's traits from this one observable event. Over a run of twenty consecutive examinations, card games, and purchases, Z also passed up eighteen opportunities to cheat. We may infer that over this range of behavior Z has a high position on a trait of resistance to cheating. So far as we know from these observations, the trait is not a very broad or general one. Further observations show that Z's conduct is similar in situations that offer opportunities for deceiving and stealing. From this information we may conclude that he is strong on a more general trait that we may call "honesty." But Z has an even more general tendency toward ethical conduct of other varieties, which justifies our placing him above the average on a still broader trait of "strength of character." Furthermore, he shows an even more general restraint or self-control that goes beyond behavior that has ethical implications, suggesting an even broader disposition or syndrome.

Because of the appearance of traits at different levels of generality, a few writers feel the need of a second type of model to supplement the first (Burt, 1949; Eysenck, 1969; Guilford, 1959a; Vernon, 1950). This is a hierarchical model, which serves to relate the factorial dimensions to one another and to a single personality. Figure 1.2 is an example of a segment of such a model.

In the illustration of traits just given, the particular acts of resistance, in whatever area of behavior—cheating, deceiving, or stealing— are at the specific-action level. Traits of cheating, of deceiving, or of stealing may be regarded as being at the "hexis" level. A hexis is

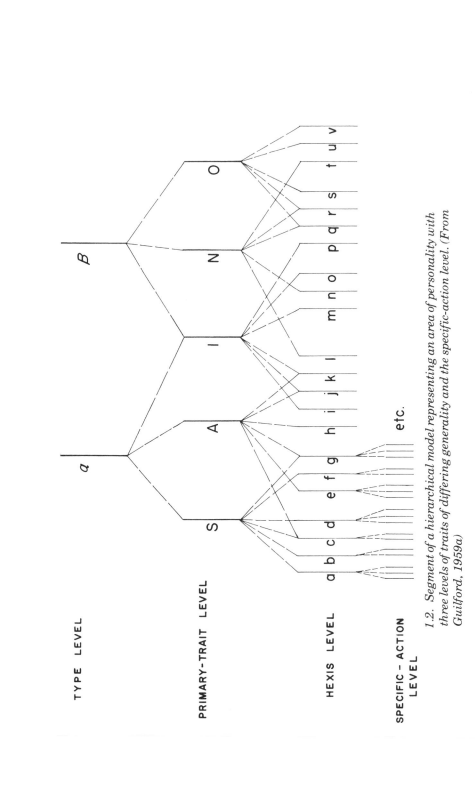

TYPE LEVEL

PRIMARY-TRAIT LEVEL

HEXIS LEVEL

SPECIFIC - ACTION LEVEL

1.2. *Segment of a hierarchical model representing an area of personality with three levels of traits of differing generality and the specific-action level. (From Guilford, 1959a)*

about the same as habit, but the term "hexis" is perferred because it is not so committed to the idea that traits are determined by learning only. A trait of honesty, for which there is factor-analytic evidence (Guilford, 1959a), may be considered to be at the primary-trait level. Strength of character and general self-restraint would be considered as syndrome types at two still higher levels.

Factor analysis can be applied at various levels in the hierarchy of traits. From information concerning intercorrelations of measured specific actions we can derive conclusions regarding the existence of unique traits at the hexis level. From intercorrelations of trait positions of individuals at the hexis level, we can derive conclusions regarding the existence of traits at the primary-trait level, and so on for higher levels. Probably most of the psychologically meaningful traits thus discovered have been at the primary-trait level.

Many of the apparent disagreements of results from different analysts should be attributed to the fact that they are analyzing at different levels in the hierarchy. The kind of factors that one obtains depends upon the level or levels at which he obtains information about individuals. In some analyses, factors of different levels are undoutedly confused.[5] From the standpoint of clarity of results, the best general strategy is to start with information at lower levels and work upward. Before we can collect clear evidence regarding unique traits at higher levels, we need to have good information about traits at lower levels.[6]

A Matrix Model. The third type of model is of more recent origin. It came about through attempts to see interrelationships among obtained factors that are probably at the primary-trait level. Although limited to one level of generality, the results could well suggest factor affiliations that would indicate higher-level traits. The logical activity is that of classification, made possible by the fact that the psychological factors within a domain possess certain similarities. But it has been found that although the traits can be put in a small number of classes, they could just as well be classified in another set of classes that cuts across the first set. For example, the known psychomotor abilities could be grouped not only according to the kind of muscular action involved, such as rate of impulsion, speed of movement, static control, precision of movement, and coordination, but also in terms of the part of the body concerned (Guilford, 1958).

---

[5]For more recently cited instances in which factors of different degrees of generality, or different levels, come out of an analysis as if they were at the same level, see Guilford, (1975).

[6]For an example of an empirically derived segment of personality in hierarchical form, see Guilford (1975).

The resulting model is a grid with a column for every type of motor ability and a row for each body part to which the kind of quality applies.

In the area of temperament, the writer has also suggested a two-dimensional model for some known factorial traits. The rows have such bipolar labels as "responsive-unresponsive," "active-passive," and "controlled-uncontrolled." The three columns have cells for the areas of behavior in which the row qualities are found, including "emotional" and "social" (Guilford, 1959a). The same source also presents a matrix of factor traits (evidently higher-order syndromes) in parallel neurotic and psychotic columns.

In the case of intellectual abilities, however, it was found necessary to construct a three-dimensional matrix (Guilford, 1959b). This is because intellectual abilities differ in three distinct ways: (1) as to kinds of operation or activity involved; (2) as to area of information being processed—that is, kind of content; and (3) as to kind of mental construct or product that must be dealt with. There are five kinds of operation, four or more kinds of content, and six kinds of product to be represented by the model. Each cell in the model is a unique interaction of one kind of operation, one kind of content, and one kind of product. The model is known as the "Structure of Intellect."[7]

In any matrix model, cells for which factor traits have not yet been demonstrated call for new directed research. The properties of such hypothesized factors are clearly indicated by their positions in the model. Another value of the model is that its class concepts are rich with potential for general theory, as will be shown. Also, the common features of each row or each column of the model can possibly serve to suggest hypotheses for higher-order factor traits to be investigated.

Factor Analysis as a Tool in Science

Factor analysis is a potent instrument for extracting information from data, but it has no magical power to reveal anything from information that is not inherent in the data. The scientist who uses the method for the discovery of psychological information should start out by asking certain questions before he collects his data. In other words, a factor-analytic study must be carefully planned, with clearly conceived hypotheses to be tested, if one is to use the method effectively.

The more experimental features the investigator can bring into his planning the better. This practice reduces ambiguity in the interpretation of results. In evaluating the scientific use of factor analysis,

---

[7]This particular model is described in the chapter that follows. For a geometric illustration of the model, see page 22.

therefore, we need to consider the kinds of hypotheses that can be adopted, the ways in which those hypotheses can be tested, the variations in conditions introduced, and the kinds of controls exerted. Many psychologists may be unaware that these experimental features are possible in factor-analytical investigations, perhaps because in publications regarding the method, so much attention is given to computational matters and so little to experimental uses of the method.

Typical Factorial Studies. Let us consider an experimental design for a factorial investigation by reference to a study of intellectual abilities. Suppose we have selected for study the area of problem solving and that we had no prior knowledge regarding factors involved in problem solving. Our first thinking about problem solving would probably suggest two hypotheses. One is that there is a single, unitary ability to solve problems, and the other is that there are a number of distinctly different abilities involved. If these were the only hypotheses that we chose to test in the first analysis, we should simply select or devise a large variety of problem-solving tasks to employ in tests. The types of problems would be widely varied, covering much range. The analysis should tell us whether one common factor is sufficient to account for all the individual differences in the problem-solving tests or whether more than one factor exists.

Let us say that the results clearly indicate that the multiple-factor hypothesis is well supported—that it takes different abilities to do well in solving problems of different types. The next study would normally be directed toward answering the question of how many factors are needed and the properties of each factor. The second study would set up hypotheses concerning the kinds of factorial abilities that should be expected. The investigator would be helped considerably by tell-tale ways in which tests clustered on common factors resulting in the first analysis, assuming that a number of mathematical factors were extracted and rotated.

From such analysis, it would appear that a factor labeled A tended to be related most to tests that call only for understanding the nature of problems—where the key to understanding is seeing relationships. A factor B is also concerned with understanding problems, but the nature of the problems is more complex—more than one relation is involved. A factor C seems concerned with thinking of solutions—with drawing conclusions. Factor D seems concerned with whether given solutions or conclusions are sound or correct.

From another point of view, certain results also tend to suggest that the kind of material in the test items—words, numbers, or pictorial material, might make some difference in how tests cluster on common factors. In the second analysis, therefore, the utilized tests were systematically varied also with respect to the kind of information in the items. Three or more tests were included in the experimental battery for each combination of specifications. Thus, it would be possible that in place of factors such as the former A, B, C, and D there could be three factors in each case rather than only one. In such a method, then, factor analysis can be applied in a hypothetico-deductive manner.

Statistical Tests and Factor Analysis. At this point the rigorously inclined investigator is quick to remind us that there are no adequate statistical tests that can be applied, either to help us decide how many common factors obtain in the particular analysis or to tell us whether factor loadings are significantly different from zero. There is no use denying this state of affairs. It is also true that there is some degree of looseness connected with rotational procedures, which contributes to uncertainty of conclusions. Conclusions must therefore be more on a permissive than a compulsive basis, even when the solution appears to be both mathematically and psychologically clear. To be completely objective, we can only say that yes, we may tolerate the idea that there is a unique psychological trait having such and such properties, or no, we cannot reasonably do so. In the latter event we may be able to conclude that there is indication of another factor, with properties not suspected before and new analysis is called for.

The reaction of some psychologists to this state of affairs may be to reject all factor-analytic results. To such a person it can be said that psychological ideas are much more important to a scientific psychologist than are statistical tests. Generally, the sciences, including psychology, originally developed and went a long way without the aid of statistical tests. The lack of statistical tests is not fatal, but the lack of psychological ideas could well be. This is not to say that we should not wish to have them both if we can do so. Until such tests become available, I suggest that we let results from factor analysis speak for themselves and that they be judged on the basis of how much they contribute to psychological understanding, prediction, and control.

Experimental Controls in Factor Analysis. To return to other experimental features of a factorial study, what conditions are systematically varied? The most conspicuous variation is in the types of tests or other experimental variables that are utilized. For the most part, these variations are qualitative. From test to test we find variations in kinds of material—figures, pictures of objects, letters, numbers, and words, to mention the most common printed forms—and we also find variations in item format—multiple-choice, matching, completion, and their derivatives. We find variations in instructions as to what is to be done and in how it is to be done.

In some instances *quantitative* variations have been introduced, such as the number of restrictions of a certain kind, the number of responses to each item, and the difficulty level of the same kind of items. One can sometimes hypothesize changes in factor loadings that should go with quantitive variations—that the loadings for a certain factor should be maximal at certain levels and minimal at others. A great deal has to be known regarding the nature of a factor before such predictions can be made, and such refinement in experimental variation can be used effectively.

Certain other conditions are at least partially controlled, or should be. The selection of the population of individuals to be used is sometimes important. In the analysis of abilities there should be relative homogeneity in age and education, and possibly in sex. Similar IQ level would be important. Ideally, the investigator should like to equate individuals with respect to a number of intellectual abilities that he might wish to exclude from consideration. But this much refinement would usually be prohibitive and fortunately it is not essential. We can tolerate such incomplete controls, for factor analysis can function without them, with its ways of segregating common-factor, specific, and error variances as parts of the entire process. This is an important distinction between multivariate and bivariate approaches.

From Factors to Functions

One of the major needs in this discussion is to establish a logical bridge between factors and general psychological theory, since factorial findings are so different from ordinary results. Previous psychological theory has arisen mainly in connection with traditional experimental approaches. In constructing the logical bridge it may help to consider some comparisons between the bivariate and multivariate approaches.

Individual Differences vs. Functioning Individuals. The main operational difference between the two approaches, in modern times, at least, is that the traditional experimentalist focuses his interest upon stimulus-response relationships. The stimulus-response model is basic to his thinking and his planning of investigations. The factorist, on the other hand, directs his attention to responses and concomitances among responses. From the intercorrelations among response values, the factorist looks for signs of traits, not for stimulus-response relations. Traits are properties of individuals. To the student of personality, their determination of behavior is just as real a phenomenon as the determination by stimuli. Some bivariate experimentalists have come to recognize this general principle, as indicated by studies of the relations of characteristic anxiety levels to various measured effects in behavior. In such an experiment, not all independent variables are stimuli, nor is any variable a temporary condition, such as mental set. A trait is used as an independent variable.

The key to the bridge is therefore the concept of "trait." In the context of personality theory, a trait is any relatively enduring way in which one person differs from others. On a scalable trait, which can be represented by a straight line, each person has a characteristic position. If individuals have different positions on a common scale, that scale represents some quality or property that each person possesses to some degree, in common with other persons. If the quality is a unique one, such as may be determined by factor analysis, it is some significant component of the individual's constitution.

There is nothing in this line of reasoning to force us to the conclusion as to the fundamental nature of this component. It might be a unique attitude, a unique motive, or a unique skill of some kind. It might be dependent upon some particular organic structure, or some combination of structures functioning together. There is nothing in ordinary factor-analytic results to tell us about the origins of a factor or to give us sufficient basis for its automatic classification.

Traits and Functions. It is easiest to see that traits imply functions in the case of abilities. Let us consider two distinct abilities in the Structure-of-Intellect model, which was mentioned earlier. One is for the cognition (knowing or understanding) of semantic (verbal) systems (such as a problem of some degree of complexity). The other is the ability to evaluate the logical soundness of an implication (deduction) when the information is in symbolic (mathematical) terms. If each person has a characteristic level of ability to perform in each of these two respects, he is certainly performing in these two ways. In other words, we may say that he has *functions* of these two types. The SI abilities may therefore be regarded as ways of functioning within individuals as well as ways in which individuals differ from one another. *Thus, from the study of how persons differ in their functioning we also learn how they are alike.*

Traits other than abilities are not so easily conceived in functional terms. Motivational traits (needs, interests, and attitudes) are not functions but are concerned with *directions* that functioning takes. Tempermental traits are concerned with the *manner* in which functioning runs its course. Thus, all kinds of psychological traits tell us about the functioning of the person as a going concern. Information regarding the factors should therefore help us to construct a picture of the behaving organism and hence contribute to psychological theory.[8]

Summary

In explaining how factor analysis and its findings can contribute to general psychological theory, this paper has described three kinds of models, derivable from factor theory or from factorial findings, that apply to personality. Personality is defined as a matter of individual differences with respect to traits. One model is a Euclidian space of n dimensions, each dimension representing a unique trait that is discoverable by factor analysis. Another model that emphasizes the structure of a typical personality represents traits at several distinct levels of generality, one of the levels being devoted to primary traits. A third kind of model arises from classification of known primary traits in columns and rows to form two- or three-dimensional matrices.

It was also thought necessary to discuss the adequacy of factor analysis as a method adaptable to the discovery of psychological concepts having theoretical significance. Used in a form of experimental design and applied to appropriate kinds of experimental variables, factor analysis can be a powerful tool for meaningful discriminations among traits. Hypothesis testing of a kind is possible, in spite of inadequate tests of statistical significance.

Although factor analysis starts with data regarding individual differences in behavior and comes out with primary traits that also refer to modes of individual differences, it is possible to deduce corresponding ways of functioning in behaving organisms. In this way we can see a bridge between factor and function or manner of functioning. The classes of factors as derived especially from the third kind of model suggest concepts that seem to have theoretical significance for psychology.

---

[8]The original paper from which this particular presentation was adapted proceeded to show how the Structure of Intellect could serve to generate theory in an "informational" psychology. References were made to areas such as learning and problem solving, to some systematic issues, and to historical points of view. These subjects are treated in much greater detail in chapters to follow.

Chapter 2

Intelligence Has Three Facets[1]

Many a layman who has taken a psychologist's intelligence test, especially if he did not do as well as he thought he should, has the conviction that a score, such as the IQ, does not tell the whole story regarding a person's level of intelligence. In thinking so, he is entirely right; traditional intelligence tests fall far short of indicating fully regarding an individual's intellectual status. Just how far short and in what respects have not been well realized until very recent years during which a broad scope of human intelligence has been intensively investigated.

This is not to say that IQ tests are not useful, for they definitely are, as years of experience have demonstrated. Intelligence tests were originated early in the century, for the purpose of determining which children could not learn at normal rates. This meant that the content of IQ tests weighted heavily those abilities that are pertinent to school learning in the key subjects of reading and arithmetic, and in other subjects that depend directly upon them or are of similar nature psychologically. IQ tests (and academic-aptitude tests) predict achievement less well at educational levels higher than the elementary grades, for at higher levels subject matter becomes more varied. Even at the elementary level, predictions of achievement have been poor in connection with the *initial* stages of learning to read, in spelling, and in the arts. The defender of IQ tests might say that intelligence is not involved in those subjects, but he would not only be wrong, he would be dodging problems.

---

[1]Based upon an article in *Science,* 1968, 615-620. Reproduced by permission.

One Intelligence or Many Abilities?

The father of IQ tests, Alfred Binet, believed firmly that intelligence is a very complex affair, comprising a number of different abilities, and he manifested this conviction by introducing tests of many different kinds into his composite scale. He did not know what the component abilities are as they are known today, although he suggested several different memory abilities, some of which were supported by much later research. Binet went along with the idea of using a single overall score, since the immediate practical goal was to make an administrative decision regarding each child.

Test makers following Binet were mostly unconcerned about having a basic psychological theory for intelligence tests, another example of technology running far in advance of theory. There was some concern about theory in England, however, where Charles Spearman developed a procedure of factor analysis by which it became possible to discover component abilities (Spearman, 1904). Spearman was obsessed with the very restricting conception that there is a universal *g* factor that is common to all tests that have any claim to the label of "intelligence tests," where each test has its own unique kind of items or problems. However, his own research, and that of some others in his country, showed that correlations between many pairs of tests could not be entirely accounted for on the basis of a single common factor (Spearman, 1927). They had to admit the existence of a number of "group" factors in addition to *g*. For example, sets of tests having verbal, numerical, or spatial material in common correlated higher within sets than they did with tests in other sets. The extra correlation of tests within sets was attributed to additional abilities, each of more limited scope.

Factor analyses in the United States have followed almost exclusively the multiple-factor theory and method of Thurstone (1935), which are more general than those of Spearman. In Thurstone's conception a *g* factor is not necessary, but analysis by his method would be likely to find it if the intercorrelations warrent such a result.

Very rarely, indeed, does anyone using the multiple-factor approach find and report a *g* factor. The reason is that there are too many zero correlations among tests of intellectual qualities, where one genuine zero coefficient would be sufficient to disallow a *g* factor that is supposed to be universal. My examination of more than 7000 intercorrelations among tests in the intellectual category showed at least 17 percent of them to be acceptable as zero correlations (Guilford, 1964). The multiple factors usually found are each restricted to only a few tests, where we may ignore factor loadings less than .30 as being insignificant, following common practice.

Discovery of Multiple Abilities

Only a few events in discovering factors by the Thurstone approach will be mentioned. In Thurstone's first major study (Thurstone, 1938) as many as nine common factors were thought to be sufficiently interpretable psychologically to justify calling them "primary mental abilities." A factor is interpreted intuitively in terms of the apparent human resource needed to do well in the set of tests loaded strongly together on the factor. A distinction between mathematical factors and psychological factors is important. Surface features of the tests in the set may differ somewhat from one another, but examinees have to perform well in some unique way to earn good scores in all of them. For example, Thurstone designated some of the abilities as being visual-perceptual, inductive, deductive, numerical, spatial, and verbal. Two others dealt with rote memory and world fluency. Thurstone and his students followed his 1938 analysis with others that revealed a few additional kinds of abilities.

Another major source of identified intellectual abilities was the research of aviation psychologists in the U. S. Army Air Force during World War II (Guilford and Lacey, 1947). More significant than the outcome of adding a few more intellectual abilities to the list was the fact that where Thurstone had found one spatial ability there proved to be at least three, one of them being recognized as spatial orientation and another as spatial visualization. In addition, where Thurstone had found one inductive ability, there were three reasoning abilities. Where Thurstone had found one memory ability, there were three, including visual memory. In some cases a Thurstone factor turned out to be a confounding of two or more separable abilities when more representative tests for the new factors were analyzed together and when allowances were made for a larger number of factors. In other cases new types of tests were explored—new memory tests, space tests, and reasoning tests.

The third major source of identified intellectual abilities was from a program of analyses conducted by the Aptitudes Research Project at the University of Southern California beginning in 1949.[1] The attention of the Project was first directed toward hypothesized abilities in the provisional categories of reasoning, creative thinking, planning, evaluation, and problem solving in general. Nearly twenty years later the number of distinct intellectual abilities was increased to about eighty,[2] and at least 50 percent more were predicted from a

---

[1] The research was supported throughout by the Personnel and Training Branch of the Office of Naval Research, with additional support at times from the U. S. Office of Education and the National Science Foundation, Biological and Medical Division.

comprehensive, unified theory. The remainder of this paper is concerned mainly with that theory.

The Structure-of-Intellect Model

Two previous attempts to put the then recognized abilities into logical schemes had been made by Burt (1949) and by Vernon (1950), with similar results. In both cases the models were of hierarchical form reminiscent of the Linnaeus taxonomic model for the animal kingdom. Following the English tradition, with its emphasis upon Spearman's *g*, that ability was placed at the apex of each system. Under *g* were broad subdivisions, under which were further subdivisions, on down to abilities considered to be very narrow in scope.

My first attempt (see Guilford, 1956) found that the hierarchical type of model had to be discarded, for several reasons. First, there had to be a rejection of *g* itself, for reasons mentioned earlier. Furthermore, most factorial abilities seemed to be of somewhat comparable level of generality, where generality is operationally defined in terms of the number of kinds of tests found to represent each ability. There appeared to be categories of abilities—some categories concerned with different types of activity, for example. Some were concerned with discovery or recognition of information, some for memory for information, some for productive thinking, and others for evaluation or judgment. There were other kinds of categories for the same abilities. The most decisive observation was that there are a number of parallels between abilities, in terms of common features.

Some examples of parallels in abilities will help. Two parallel abilities differ in only one respect. There is known to be an ability to see relations between pairs of perceived, visual figures, and an ability to see relations between pairs of concepts. An example of a test item in the first case would require the examinee to see that one figure is the lower left half of the other. An item in the second case might be to require seeing that the words "bird" and "fly" refer to an object and its mode of transportation or its activity. The ability to do the one kind of item is relatively independent of the ability to do the other, the only difference being the kind of information—concrete in the one case and abstract or conceived in the other.

For a pair of abilities differing in another way, the kind of information is the same for both. For example, one ability pertains to seeing class ideas. Given the set of words *footstool, lamp, rocker, television,* can the examinee grasp the nature of the class, as shown by naming

---

[2]At the termination of the Project in 1969, the number of demonstrated factorial abilities reached the century mark. Other hypothesized abilities had not been investigated.

the class, by putting another word or two into the class, or by recognizing the class name among four alternatives? The ability pertains to discovery or recognition of a class concept among meaningful materials. In another kind of test we ask the examinee to construct classes by partitioning a list of words into mutually exclusive sets, each with a different class concept. The two abilities are relatively independent, and two different psychological processes are involved. The one involves a process of understanding and the other a process of production.

A third kind of parallel-abilities test has pairs of items of information that are alike and also the same kind of operation. Suppose we give this kind of item: "Name as many objects as you can that are both white and edible." Here we have given the specifications for a class and the examinee is to produce from his memory store some class members. The ability involved was first called "ideational fluency." The more appropriate class members the examinee gives in limited time the better his score. In a test for a parallel ability, instead of producing single words the examinee is to generate a list of short sentences. In order to standardize his task for testing purposes and to further control his efforts, we give him the initial letters of four words that he is to give in a variety of sentences, for example: W_____ c_____ s_____ d_____. Without using any word twice, the examinee might say, "Why can't Susan dance?," "Workers could seldom deviate," or "Weary cats sense destruction." The ability was at first called "expressional fluency." The kind of information in both tests is conceptual, and the kind of operation is production.

It should be noted that the kind of *operation* involved in the last two tests is different from that of the test mentioned earlier that required sorting objects into classes. That test required the examinee to come out with one particular set of classes; the operation was convergent production. In the last two tests the examinee branches out in different directions, so the operation is called "divergent production." The one kind of task requires a zeroing in on a particular outcome whereas the other requires a broad search or scanning of the memory store for a variety of items of information.

The difference between the two abilities illustrated by the last two illustrative tests is in the nature of the things produced. In the first case they are in the form of single words that stand for single objects or ideas. The thing produced, the "product," is a *unit*. In the second case the product is an organized sequence of words or units. It is therefore a *system*.

In order to take care of all such parallels (and the number increased as time went on and experience grew in the Aptitudes Research Project), a matrix type of model seemed called for, in the manner of Mendeleev's table of chemical elements. The differences between abilities in the three ways indicated—operation (kind of processing procedure), content (substantive kind of information), and product (form that information takes)—called for a three-dimensional model. As presented in 1959 (Guilford, 1959b), the Structure of Intellect had five categories of operation, four of content, and six of product (see Figure 2.1).[2]

It is readily seen that the theory called for $5 \times 4 \times 6$, or 120, cells in the model, each one representing a unique ability by virtue of its peculiar conjunction of operation, content, and product. In illustrations of abilities already given, the reader has been introduced to three kinds of operation: cognition (discovery, recognition, comprehension), divergent production, and convergent production. The memory operation involves putting information into memory storage with some degree of permanence. It must be distinguished from the memory store itself. The latter underlies all operations; all abilities depend upon it. This is a logical basis for believing that abilities increase with experience. The operation of evaluation deals with assessment of information, either cognized or produced, determining its goodness with respect to adopted logical criteria, such as identity and consistency.

The distinction between figural and semantic information was mentioned earlier. Figural information has sensory properties, such as visual or auditory. It is often regarded as "concrete," whereas semantic information is abstract. The latter is called "semantic" because it is ordinarily attached to words symbols, but this connection is not essential; we have imageless thoughts that we cannot put into words. The recognition of symbolic information came later than the recognition of figural and semantic information. Tests of symbolic abilities commonly use letters or numbers, but other signs that have only token value could be used. The symbolic code is the primary basis for mathematics.

The category of behavioral information was added on the basis of a hunch; no abilities involving it were known to have been demonstrated when it was included. One basis was E. L. Thorndike's (1920) suggestion that there is a "social intelligence," distinct from what he called "concrete" and "abstract" intelligences. It was decided to distinguish "social intelligence" on the basis of kind of information, or content. This is the kind of information that a person derives form observations of the behavior of another. From expressive signs, or "body language," one can become aware of the attention, feelings,

---

[2]The most recent version of the model includes a fifth content category, the figural category having been divided into visual and auditory areas (Guilford, 1977a). Other sensory areas may have to be added after they have been investigated in the same manner.

2.1. *The Structure-of-Intellect model (in its original form).*

thoughts, and intentions of another person. Subsequent investigations demonstrated a full set of six behavioral-cognition abilities as predicted by the model, and a current analytical investigation is designed to test the part of the model that includes six behavioral-divergent-production abilities.

In one test designed for the cognition of behavioral systems, three parts of a four-part cartoon are given in each item, with four alternative parts that are potential completions. The examinee has to size up the situation in each item (to cognize a behavioral system) and to select the appropriate part to complete the system. As a test for divergent production of behavioral systems the examinee is given descriptions of three characters, for example, a jubilant man, an angry woman, and a sullen boy, for which he is to construct a number of alternative story plots involving the characters and their moods, all stories being different.

Four kinds of products have already been illustrated: units, classes, relations, and systems. The other two kinds of products are transformations and implications. Transformations include any kind of change: movement in space, rearrangement or regrouping letters in words or simplifying an equation, redefining a word or adapting an object to a new use, or revising one's interpretation of another person's action or rearranging events in a story. In these examples four kinds of informational content are involved, from visual-figural to behavioral, illustrating the fact that all six kinds of products apply in every content category for any kind of operation.

Implied information is suggested by other information. Foresight or prediction depends upon extrapolating from given information to some naturally following condition or event. If I make this move in chess my knight will be vulnerable. If I divide by x I will have a simpler expression. If it rains tonight my tent will leak. If I whistle at that girl she will turn her head. The "If . . . then" expression well describes an implication.

Some Consequences of the Theory

The most immediate consequence of the theory and its model has been its heuristic value in suggesting where to look to find still undemonstrated abilities. From the beginning, the modus operendi of the Aptitudes Research Project had been to hypothesize certain kinds of abilities, to create new types of tests that should emphasize each hypothesized ability, then to factor analyze in order to determine whether the hypotheses were well supported. With hypotheses generated from the model, the rate of demonstration of new abilities was much accelerated.

Having developed a comprehensive and systematic theory of intelligence, it was found that not the least of its benefits is an entirely new point of view in psychology generally, a view that has been called "operational-informational." Information is defined for psychology as that which the organism discriminates. Without discrimination there is no information. This view is in line with that of communication engineers. Without carrying the comparison further, let it be said that the psychologist's information is transmitted information.

Psychological discriminations are first of all along the lines of the kinds of content and kinds of products of the Structure-of-Intellect model from which arise the hiatuses among intellectual abilities. Further discriminations occur, of course, within the sphere of each single ability. I have proposed that the 4 × 6 intersections of the informational categories of the model provide a psycho-epistemology, with twenty-four subcategories of basic information. I have also proposed that the six product categories—units, classes, relations, systems, transformations, and implications—provide the basis for a psycho-logic (Guilford, 1967). Most of these terms are familiar ones in modern formal logic. All are clearly demonstrated in mathematics.

The operational-informational view regards the organism as a processor of information, for which the modern electronic computer is a good analogy. From this point of view, the computer-simulation studies make sense. But there are limits to the analogies between functions. Although a psychology based upon SI concepts is much more complicated than the stimulus-response model that had at one time become traditional, it is still parsimonious, with only fifteen basic categories. It has a better chance of becoming an adequate interpreter of behavior. The Structure of Intellect, as such, is a taxonomic model. In telling us *what* exists it provides useful concepts. For theory that accounts for behavior we also need operational models some of which have already been suggested (Guilford, 1967).

Some Special Findings

Two examples can be given briefly here to help clarify the way in which SI concepts apply in accounting for some well-known mental activities—problem solving and creative thinking.

The research on abilities well demonstrated the fact that there is no one problem-solving ability. Many different SI abilities may be drawn upon in solving a problem, depending upon the nature of the problem. Almost always there are cognitive operations (in seeing that a problem exists and in understanding the nature of the problem), productive operations (in generating steps toward solution), and evaluative operations (in checking upon both cognitive and productive activities). Memory operations enter in to keep a running record of information regarding previous steps. And the memory store of information underlies all.

Finally, there is something novel about the solutions to problems, hence creative thinking is involved. Creative thinking depends mostly upon divergent production operations on the one hand and on products of transformation on the other. Thus, these two categories have unique roles in creative thinking and problem solving. There is, accordingly, no one unique ability to account for creative potential. Creative production depends upon the area in which one works, whether it is in pictorial art, music, drama, mathematics, science, writing, or management. In view of the relative independence of the intellectual abilities, unevenness of the status in the various abilities of the same individual should be the rule rather than the exception. Some individuals should excel in more than one art form, but few excel in all. A case in point is the practice of having many creative contributors to the production of a single motion picture.

Summary

By intensive factor-analytic investigations, mostly in the past twenty years, the multiple-factor picture of intelligence has grown far beyond the expectations of those most concerned. A comprehensive, systematic theoretical model known as the "Structure of Intellect" has been developed to put order and rationality into the picture.

The model is a cubical affair, its three dimensions representing ways in which the abilities differ from one another. Represented are five kinds of operations, four substantive kinds of information or "contents," and six formal kinds of information or "products," respectively. Each intellectual ability involves a unique conjunction of one kind of operation, one kind of content, and one kind of product. All abilities appear to be relatively independent in a population, but appear with common joint involvement in intellectual activity.

Chapter 3

Executive Functions

and a Model of Behavior[1]

In a program of research on intelligence during a twenty-year interval, The Aptitudes Research Project at the University of Southern California devoted its efforts to the differentiation of abilities, which were assumed to indicate unique functions of the information-processing human organism, at least in European-American culture (Guilford, 1967; Guilford & Hoepfner, 1971). In one of the last factor-analytic investigations, there appeared serendipitously two factors that were interpreted as belonging to a quite different category, heretofore hypothesized (Guilford, 1967) but never reported. It is the purpose of this paper to introduce these variables of personality and to suggest the significance of functions of this kind for behavior in general. They were identified as "executive" functions, because they seem to be concerned with intentions and with initiation and management of motor responses.

A Demonstration of Executive Functions

The primary purpose of the investigation in question was to test the hypothesis that the six behavioral-divergent-production abilities projected by the writer's Structure-of-Intellect (SI) model could be demonstrated. Behavioral abilities, to that time, were concerned with the processing of information that we have of the mental states of other individuals from what we can perceive of their expressive actions, including speech. Divergent production is the operation of

[1]Reprinted with permission from the *Journal of General Psychology*, 1972, 86, 279-287.

generating logical alternatives in response to given information. Six abilities were hypothesized, to correspond to the kinds of psychological products of the SI model—units, classes, relations, systems, transformations, and implications.

An Analysis of Expressive Tests. In the main analysis, according to customary practice, three to five tests were designed to represent each expected factor, for example, divergent production of behavioral units or divergent production of behavioral implications. The tests were designed for group administration, hence they were in printed form, and the examinee (*S*) gave written answers, verbal and nonverbal, to report their behavioral ideas.

In order to broaden the scope of the investigation, a minor study was added in order to determine whether the factors that might emerge would also be exhibited when other than written responses were used. Natural alternatives to written responses were expressive-behavioral actions. Two kinds of expressive responses were used: facial and vocal.[2] Given a specified behavioral event, in the first case *S* was to produce a number of facial expressions, all appropriate to the event and all different. In the second case he was to produce a number of vocal expressions, also all appropriate and all different. There were two tests of the first type and two of the second. The facial-expression responses were photographed, and the vocal-expression responses were tape-recorded. In every test the score was the total number of non-duplicating appropriate responses given to the items.

In a special study, the four expressional tests were factor analyzed along with a few printed tests, in a special sample of *S*s. A few words are in order regarding the nature of both the printed and the expressive tests in this analysis. Four of the printed tests were designed for SI ability DBU (divergent production of behavioral units), where a unit is a particular mental state, such as doubt, dread, or friendliness. In each item of Alternate Picture Meanings, a line drawing is given of a face or some other body part in some kind of pose—a man's head, bowed and with thumb and forefinger astride his nose, for example. In Alternate Social Meanings, a behavioral event is stated, such as "One person winks at another." The task is to give a number of different statements as to what the person is thinking or feeling. In Multiple Emotional Expressions, a single emotion is named ("disgust," for example) and *S* is to write a number of statements that a disgusted person might say. Expressing Mixed Emotions asks what a person might say if he were beset with two different emotions—if he

---

[2]This experiment was in direct charge of Dr. Ralph Hoepfner, with the assistance of Mr. Richard Martin.

were both angry and amused, for instance. In a much larger analysis with printed tests only, these tests performed as expected, loading strongly on the same factor that was identified as DBU.

One of the facial-response tests presented only a single short statement in each problem (such as, "You have to leave now,") and S was to produce a number of different expressions to go with the statement. Problems of the other facial test described a stituation to provide a background for a statement—for example, "You and your friend are at a circus watching a trapeze act, and you say to your friend, 'Look at what's happening.' " In other problems in the same test, other settings were presented along with the same remark.

The given information for the two vocal-expression tests was very similar. An example of a single sentence is, "I'm going to do it." An example of a specified situation with a specified statement to be uttered by S reads, "You have just heard some wonderful news and you say to your friend, 'I can hardly believe it.' "

It was thought that if the expressive tests did load on any of the behavioral-divergent-production factors, it would be the one for DBU, because each expression refers to a single item in an expressive vocabulary. Printed tests expected to represent two divergent-production abilities (DBC and DBR) were included in the small factor analysis, but they are of no concern to us here. Nine printed tests and the four expressive tests were administered individually to volunteer students, thirty-four of whom completed all tests. A factor analysis based upon so small a sample is ordinarily not to be recommended, but the time and effort involved in individual testing, and the clear-cut nature of the results, justify attention to the findings.

The factor analysis, with extraction of principal axes and with varimax rotations, yielded the factor matrix shown in Table 3.1, with only the pertinent data given. From the given data, it is obvious that the printed and expressive tests had practically nothing in common. It had been expected that there would be at least some relationship because in both cases S should be producing a variety of behavioral ideas in each problem, with only the medium of communication differing. But the decisive results indicate otherwise. Whatever production of behavioral ideas may occur in responding to the expressive tests, variance from individual differences in this respect must be minimal. The problem solutions in the expressive tests are dependent upon something quite different, and that something must be in the mobilization of motor patterns to create the expressions. Such a mobilization would seem to satisfy a conception of executive activity; a putting into effect of organized motor innervation. In the case of printed tests, there was none of this kind of problem, for writing is a general-purpose mode of expression and a highly practiced skill, decidedly overlearned.

Granting that executive functions account in part for individual differences in the expressive tests, the results of the analysis tell us, further, that two distinctly different functions were involved in facial and vocal expressions. Apparently, we have a facial executive function and a vocal executive function, and abilities in their operations are independent, or nearly so. This conclusion is supported by the fact that input information in the two cases was much the same. The differentiation was therefore on the motor side of the behaving organism. An important implication is that those who would seek to establish a taxonomy of executive functions should expect to find them differentiated in terms of muscle groups, as well as kinds of motor patterns.

Table 3.1   Rotated Factor Matrix for Four Printed
Tests of Behavioral Divergent Production and Four
Expressive Tests

Tests	Factor Loadings		
	DMU	Facial	Vocal
Alternate Picture Meanings	79	−.02	.24
Alternate Social Meanings	.71	−.13	.19
Multiple Emotional Expressions	.67	.21	.01
Expressing Mixed Emotions	.41	−.04	.25
Facial (sentence only)	.16	.56	−.02
Facial (sentence and situation)	.07	.78	.30
Vocal (sentence only)	.06	.09	.73
Vocal (sentence and situation)	−.08	.06	.79

The Nature of Executive Functions

In explication of the nature of executive functions, the writer can hardly do better than to quote from his first proposal of the concept (Guilford, 1967, p. 293):

On the basis of input information and central operations with it, a general command is issued to the effector system. The command might be "Look in the morning newspaper to see what the Dodgers did in the game last night." This statement describes the main goal of the act, which calls into play a number of subgoals, including hunting for the newspaper, picking it up, turning to the sports section, and finding the appropriate column. Each of these part actions, in turn, calls into play subsidiary movements. Picking up the newspaper involves reaching, grasping, and lifting. Turning to the sports section involves possible looking at the index on the front page, separating the sections of the newspaper, and grasping the two edges preparatory to reading. Finding the right column involves looking at various headlines. The total action is made up of a hierarchical organization of subactions and subsidiary movements.

The permanent memory store . . . [contains] different levels of executive systems of different degrees of generality. In the course of development, the infant learns the detailed elements of movement first, in the form of waving, pushing, pulling, grasping, clapping, clutching, pinching, releasing, throwing, lifting, holding, dropping, shoving, and so on. Such events may be regarded as *units* of executive information. *Classes* are formed by virtue of the fact that collections of different movements have similar effects, such as increasing the distance between the object and the person, as in pushing, shoving, repelling, rejecting, and so on, which can be done with one hand or the other, with legs, or with the head. *Systems* are formed by combining pieces of action into patterns and by producing hierarchical arrangements. There are possibilities of applying other (SI) product categories to movements. For example, a *transformation* would occur when a particular movement is adapted to some new use or when a system is reorganized. An *implication* would apply where one movement naturally leads to another.

Thus, its seems possible to say that the kinds of products of information that apply to cognized information also apply in the area of psychomotor activity. It may be said that it is this kind of parallel that has much to do with the translation of cognition into motor action. The isomorphism between the two stages of behavior goes even further in bridging the gap in more detailed ways. Also, on the side of cognition, the individual builds up considerable information concerning his own reacting equipment, its potential and its limitations. The individual has in his memory store information regarding his action equipment, what it can do and what it cannot do, and there is information concerning which equipment is best used for different purposes. On the side of cognition, this line of thinking presupposes heavy involvement of abilities or functions for processing kinesthetic information. There is already evidence for one kinesthetic ability (Guilford, 1967).[3]

---

[3]The systems involved in executive functioning, and perhaps other products, may be very close to conceptions of "plans" that were suggested by Miller, Galanter, and Pribram (1960).

An Operational-Informational Model of Behavior

The writer has previously presented an operational model to represent a generic conception of problem solving (Guilford, 1967), which is based upon SI operations and kinds of information. He also presented a form of Crossman's (1964) detailed operational model for intentions and executions of overt actions. Both models pertain to the transmission of information in various ways. A natural next step was to put the two models together, in somewhat condensed form, in order to achieve a more complete picture of behavior that extends from stimulus input to motor output. The model is shown in Figure 3.1. It enables us to see where executive functions fit into the total information-processing picture.

The model represents a complete behavioral action, beginning with sensory input and ending with motor output, although in some instances behavioral activity may not be complete. In a complete action, the stimulus may originate from the environment or from the soma of the individual, or both. The filter (see Figure 3.1) is concerned with attention, both with respect to arousal or vigilance and to its selective aspect. The operations of cognition, production (divergent and convergent), and evaluation are as defined in the Structure-of-Intellect theory. The memory store, however, is not to be identified with the *operation* of memory. The latter is a matter of putting information into storage, a process that is represented in the model by the arrows pointing toward the memory store. The memory store is shown as receiving information from all the operations, including those of execution and motor functioning. It is the record keeper and the supplier of information from past experiences. Everywhere, it has double transactions with the functions. It even affects the filtering operaton, but there is no reason to show that filtering processes, as such, are put into memory storage. This kind of event is not inconceivable, but it is more clearly the things passed through the filter that are put into storage.

Another ubiquitous aspect of the model is the operation of evaluation. As stated in a number of places previously, this operation is a cybernetic function involving matching of output with input at any stage of behavior. Such a process evidently applies to the operations of the executive and motor functions. Everywhere, things ordinarily proceed under the checking and guidance of evaluation. A notable exception is a bypassing of evaluation, indicated by the arrows going directly from the memory store to the various operational stages. Impulsive actions would be in this category, as well as an activity in the well-known "brainstorming" technique in problem solving. On other occasions, the urgency of a crisis demands this kind of short-circuiting. Other kinds of short-circuiting will also be pointed out.

The motor functions have not yet been accounted for in this discussion. They are the more restricted neuromuscular events that are demanded by executive functions and follow from them. Their distinction from the executive functions, as such, is supported by historical findings of psychomotor factorial abilities, which appear to have nothing to do with intentions, particular organizations of movements, or directing of movements. Psychomotor abilities are concerned with such properties as speed, both speed of initiation of muscular movement, as in reaction-time tests, and speed of movement after initiation of movement. Another major class of psychomotor abilities has to do with precision of muscular control. There is precision in holding bodily positions, as in steadiness tests (static precision), and there is precision in action, as in aiming tests (dynamic precision). Other kinds of abilities pertain to strength, coordination, and flexibility.

Psychomotor abilities are also differentiated in terms of the part of the body involved—trunk, limbs, hands, and fingers (perhaps also vocal organs). The writer has constructed a matrix type of model for the psychomotor abilities, which finds places for all the known abilities of this type and predicts more abilities that should be found by appropriate analyses (Guilford, 1958). It is the existence of this model and of the SI model for intellectual abilities that suggests a potentially fruitful field for investigations of executive abilities by factor analysis, aimed at still another taxonomy.

An important feature of the model for behavior is the large amount of short-circuiting that it recognizes. Following William James's early treatment of habit formation, functional psychologists frequently held to the principal that in the early stages of learning there is considerable conscious content, which progressively drops out as a habit becomes more automatized. The model makes one important conceptual gain by substituting "information" for "consciousness." Information is a much more specifiable and manageable concept, in step with much current thinking. In a behavioral event that includes motor output, all the operations indicated between stimulus and response may be involved. This is particularly true when problem solving is needed. In successive encounters with similar situations, the needs for productive operations are likely to be the first to disappear, changing the routing from line f to line e in Figure 3.1. As the act comes to be performed without intention, the executive functions also drop out, and route d comes into play. Further automatizing would involve routes c, b, and even a, a route that applies to reflex actions.

Although these conceptions in a sense revive old views, it is important to note that by the recognition of the various kinds of intervening operations—intellectual, executive, and motor—attention is called to points at which to direct research. In the changes occurring

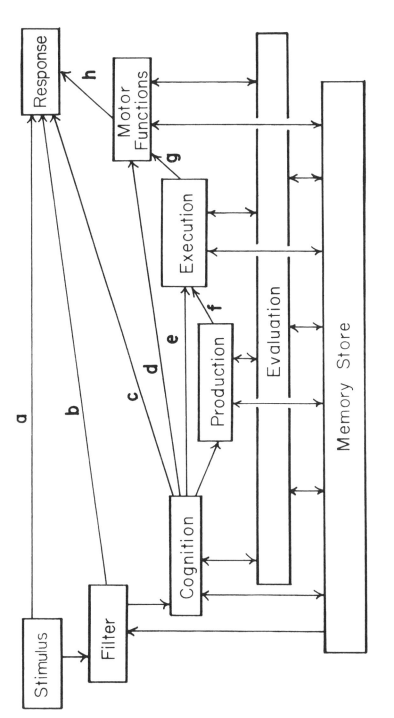

3.1. A model of behavior, including both intellectual and motor functions.

during the formation of complex habits or skills, we know where to look for modifications of behavior. It is significant, also, that we have been led to the conception of this model by virtue of the taxonomies that have been derived from experimental application of factor analysis to data regarding individual differences. Further taxonomic investigations should be very helpful in making future progress.

It must be recognized that the model of behavior proposed here is by no means complete. Most obviously lacking are references to motivational aspects of the behaving person. There would seem to be no insurmountable obstacles in conceiving of those aspects of behavior also in terms of information transmission. The information involved pertains to the person himself, which suggests that there might be an additional slab in the Structure-of-Intellect model, another kind of content, devoted to self-generated behavioral information. Something in addition may be needed. However this may be, if one judges from the steps by which the model of Figure 3.1 was achieved, it appears that efforts should be directed toward development of a taxonomy, or taxonomies, in the areas of motivation, feeling, and emotion.

Summary

Evidence was presented for the existence of distinguishable abilities or functions involved with intentions and the initiation and organization of motor components of behavior. The empirical basis was the factor-analytic discovery of abilities concerned with the production of facial and vocal expressions of emotions appropriate to given situations. The role of executive functions in complete behavioral events was indicated by placing them in an information-transmission model of behavior, by combining a problem-solving model with an efferent-process model. Forms of short-circuiting that are related to learning were pointed out.

Chapter 4

A Psychology with Act

Content, and Form[1]

Almost from the inception of the Structure-of-Intellect (SI) theory and model, I have urged the view that its concepts have considerable promise as a basis for general psychological theory (Guilford, 1959a). The most definitive treatments of the SI model may be found in either of two volumes (Guilford, 1967; Guilford & Hoepfner, 1971).

Step by step, the implications of the SI model for psychological theory have been elaborated in various ways. By 1965 it was realized that the *kinds of information* represented in the model contribute a very important basis for understanding intellectual functioning, including the four kinds of content—figural, symbolic, semantic, and behavioral—and the six kinds of products—units, classes, relations, systems, transformations, and implications (Guilford, 1966). In this connection, it was proposed that the products could furnish the basis for a psycho-logic, and the twenty-four kinds of information generated by multiplication of four contents times six products provides a psycho-epistemology.

The suggestion was also made that the ancient and honorable concept of association should be replaced in psychological theory by the product of implication. The concept of implication stresses the logical nature of connections between things, logical in the sense that there are meaningful reasons for connections between items of information, such as cause and effect, expectations, belongingness, and so on. It was also pointed out that there are five other forms of

[1]Reproduced with permission from the *Journal of General Psychology,* 1974, 90, 87-100, with minor editorial changes and with a new Summary.

information—the five other products—to provide a much broader vocabulary for describing mental events.

Psychological variables derived from factor analysis, and the class concepts that they generate, are taxonomic affairs. In order to put them to work in psychological theory it is necessary to apply them to ongoing events. My first attempt in this direction was in a presentation on learning theory as seen from an operational-informational (OI) point of view (Guilford, 1960a). Later, an operational model for problem solving was proposed (Guilford, 1966). In a volume largely devoted to psychological theory, the same general view was applied to perception, learning, memory, and creative thinking, as well as to problem solving (Guilford, 1967). Some possible applications of OI concepts to motivation and affective processes were treated in a Nebraska Symposium on Motivation (Guilford, 1965). More recently, psychomotor output activities were brought into the general OI picture in presenting the concept of "executive functions" and a general outline model for behavior (Guilford, 1972).

It is the purpose of this paper to take a larger view; to consider relations of an OI psychology to some of the major issues in the history of theoretical psychology, with some comparisons with historical points of view. It will be maintained that an OI point of view provides a more complete framework than has yet been realized in any one system of psychology. Because of its relative completeness, it offers a good vantage point from which to evaluate the historical psychologies. A good framework requires all three aspects— operations, contents, and forms. Every historical view has fallen short in one or more of these respects. In fact, most points of view restricted themselves very much to only one of the dimensions of the SI model. Even within one of those dimensions there have been further limitations, as will be pointed out. At the same time, in piecemeal manner, some precursors for SI concepts can be found.

Content Psychologies

It is commonly agreed that modern, scientific psychology got its start with philosophers who, perpetually concerned with problems of knowledge, saw in the empirical approach of the sensory physiologists a way for solving their problems. Already the physiologists who dealt with the senses and perception were demonstrating how human knowledge is gained through sensory avenues. The philosophers' attention was therefore turned toward conscious experience as the subject matter to be observed.

Wundtian Psychology. Wundt recognized three basic kinds of content—sensations, images, and feelings. He thought that the psychologist's task was to observe these aspects of mental events and to arrive at principles to account for complex manifestations of content, such as ideas, intentions, and emotions. In doing this, Wundt and his followers had at their disposal, from its cultivation by the British psychologists, the principle of association, but they never used it effectively to meet their problems of accounting for complex events in terms of combinations of elements.

Wundt's disciple, Titchener, both simplified and elaborated the Wundtian conceptions of mental content (Titchener, 1929). Simplification took the form of reducing images and feelings to sensations. He held that images are simply revived or reproduced sensations, having only sensory properties. In his laboratory it was concluded that when feelings are closely examined, they are actually somatic or bodily sensations. Titchener's step toward elaboration was to say that all sensations have in common a number of attributes, which can contribute to a great variety of experiential events. The elaborations did little or nothing to solve the problems of knowledge, but Titchener thought that as a scientist he had passed well beyond that goal.[2]

In terms of the four kinds of SI content, it is clear that the so-called structuralists or existentialists recognized only one kind of information, namely figural, but figural information of all sense modalities to be sure. Up to the present, of all the sense modalities, factor-analytic investigations have been very much restricted to visual-figural information and to auditory-figural information, on which little has been done. It seems possible to extend analysis of this kind to any sense modality that is at all structured.

Titchener vigorously rejectd from his psychology all meaning, as such, thus shunning semantic information, such as is given a place in the SI model. By means of his context theory, Titchener thought that he had successfully accounted for the occurrence of meaning by observing sensations that accompany each meaning event. Now it is true that the individual, as a processor of information, can and does engage in much translating from one SI content to another, as when the abstract idea of justice is represented by balanced scales. But such a substitution does not deny the occurrence of an abstract idea (semantic item of information), nor do we need to rule out meaning, as such, from psychology. The SI semantic category is designed to take care of that.[3]

As for the other SI content categories, Wundt and Titchener had no

---

[2]Titchener maintained that problems of knowledge belong to epistemology, not to psychology, a view that contemporary congitive psychologists would definitely reject.

[3]It may be of interest to note at this point that the author of this paper has imitated Titchener in his context theory of meaning by developing another context theory that accepts not only figural (sensory) but also other kinds of SI content in the context of a particular semantically conceived concept. (Guilford, 1967).

place for symbolic information, but it may be said that Wundt took a step in the direction of behavioral information when he adopted feelings as basic kinds of consciousness. Thus, we can say that the psychologies of Wundt and Titchener were very much restricted, not only to content but also to one kind of content—sensory, which is to say, figural.

Imageless-Thought Psychology. There were a few content psychologists who took limited steps in the direction of other SI categories. The important center for this activity was at Würzburg, in the school of imageless thought, with Ach, Messer, Marbe, and others. Dissatisfied with the Wundtian limitation to sensations and other elements, in their investigations of thinking processes they saw the need for something in addition. They came to recognize such psychological phenomena as mental attitudes (*Bewusstseinslagen*) and cognitions (*Bewusstheiten*). In their general concept of "imageless thoughts" they were evidently referring to semantic content. Some of their reported *Bewusstheiten* are like SI semantic products (relations, systems, and implications). They reported observations of relations. They reported awareness of problems, which are commonly semantic systems. Their sets and expectations were probably concerned with implications. But in spite of these extensions of kinds of information, they were a long way from covering the twenty-four-category epistemology of the SI model.

One of Titchener's criticisms of the Würzburg psychologists, and others, was that they tended to leave psychology and to go in the direction of epistemology or logic (Titchener, 1929). From the SI model, we see that psychology actually needs an epistemology, and we see that information can be handled scientifically, no matter what its category. In Titchener's conception of science, only directly observed experience can be tolerated as a basis for psychological observation and theory. When the Würzburgers said they were actually observing meanings, Titchener declared that they were not observing but simply reporting that meanings had occurred. These views represent an issue as to what constitutes an observation and a description in science. The Würzburgers did liberalize the concept of "description," but they could legitimately have gone much further.

Incidentally, they did not realize it, but the Würzburgers were an important source of the psychological test. The tasks or problems that they gave to their observers were like test items of more recent times. Two important steps were needed for putting those tasks in the category of mental tests. One step was to standardize the items of the task and the conditions under which it was given, and the other was to use a score representing goodness of performance as the observation rather than the problem solver's report of what transpired in his thinking. It remained for factor analysis to derive from test scores some information that points to the kind of functioning that occurs during mental work on a task. The analysis starts with objectively observed information, the test scores, but comes out with what might be called inferential descriptions, where observations are indirect. The factor analyst may use introspective observations as an aid to interpretation of factors, but this is probably not necessary, as inferential observations are tolerated in the best of sciences. It has taken a long time for psychologists, shaky about their own status as scientists, to accept inferential descriptions. Some are still loath to do so.

Psychoanalytic Psychology. It may seem at first surprising to consider the psychoanalysts as content psychologists, but in one sense this is true. We may say that they have dealt with the SI model's behavioral information only. But their concerns have been with *what* individuals think and feel, not in *how* those processes run their course or what their fundamental nature is. In this respect they have stood apart from the mainstream of psychological theory.

It must be recognized that psychoanolysis is also an act psychology, for it deals with ongoing events, and there is an emphasis on the "dynamic." But, again, there is little interest in understanding the fundamental nature of ways in which information is processed, any more than there is in the nature of information, in ways that would achieve an SI type of model. Psychoanalysis has been concerned primarily with affective rather than intellectual aspects of mental functioning, trying, in its way, to fill the enormous gap left by traditional psychologists.

Operational Psychologies

The "operation" or "act" psychologists are the oldest, if we accept the faculty psychologists of ancient origin as belonging to that category. Although the mental faculties were conceived as "powers," or dispositions of readiness to perform in certain ways, there are naturally parallel kinds of manifested activities or functions. Although modern psychologists violently rejected such ancestry, the more commonly recognized faculties (memory, attention, and reasoning, for example) frequently became chapter headings.

Faculty Psychology. The main justifiable criticism of faculty psychology is that it lacked empirical methods, such as factor analysis, for testing its hypothesized traits or functions. It did offer taxonomies in its lists of faculties. But in place of a unitary power or function of reasoning, I have proposed that the twenty-four SI cognition abilities replace the concept of inductive reasoning, and that the twenty-four convergent-production abilities replace the concept of deduction (Guilford, 1960b).

The SI model calls for twenty-four varieties of memory (Guilford, 1971), and there is evidence for perhaps twice that number, since some hiatus between short-term and long-term memory abilities has been recently indicated by factor analysis (Kamstra, 1971). The faculty of judgment may be replaced by the twenty-four evaluation abilities, and where there was a faculty of imagination, we may now look to the twenty-four divergent-production abilities.

Act Psychologies. In the act psychologies of Brentano and his followers, we should also look for precursors of the SI operation categories. Among other things, Brentano recognized two broad classes of acts— ideating and judging. The former was described as if it included the three SI operations of cognition and divergent and convergent production. Brentano's act of judging seems equivalent to the SI operation of evaluation.

Although the act psychologists defined an act as "intentional," in the sense that every act "intends" or points to an object, it paid little or no attention to the object as content. With such an intimate connection conceived between act and content, it should have been natural to classify acts according to kinds of content as well as kinds of operation. This would have brought one or more other dimensions of the SI model into the picture. But this was not the case.

Functional Psychologies. The need for informational concepts seems evident in the functional psychology of Stumpf (1906), who came nearer to recognizing both contents and products. His acts of perception can be equated to figural-cognition abilities of the SI model. His act of "grouping" suggests either divergent or convergent production of classes, thus referring at least implicitly to an SI product. His construct of "conception" was described as if it were semantic content. His act of "judgment," like Brentano's, suggests evaluation. Some of these apparent parallels indicate how badly Stumpf needed to see more clearly that there are content and product categories. He tried to fit everything into operations only.

Reference to Stumpf's psychology as being functional suggests American functionalism as another primarily operational form of psychology. Although the label indicates an attempt to get away from a purely content psychology, the functional concepts were borrowed largely from faculty psychology, and there were attempts to read biological utility, more particularly Darwin's principle of survival value, into mental activities, There was a latent distinction between act and content, but very few further distinctions in the direction of SI categories.

Behaviorism. Like psychoanalysis, behaviorism has been somewhat off the initial mainstream of modern psychology. Insofar as it fits into that mainstream, it is best classified as an act psychology. Its acts, of course, are observable, overt stimulus-response sequences. It has had very little to say about events intervening between stimulus and response, which have been the phenomena of primary concern in the history of psychology.

The only clear link that can be seen to SI conceptions lies in the principle of association, which, in SI interpretation, is a matter of implication. In a conditioned response, the SI interpretation would be that one item of information (from the conditioned stimulus) comes to imply another (from the unconditioned stimulus). This interpretation is equivalent to Tolman's expectation conception of conditioning.

Taking a purely behavioristic view, one might also say that conditioned stimuli come to imply responses. Putting the matter this way suggests that the nervous system is a logical device in whatever it does. It was said earlier that all the SI products are logical matters. Thus, the behaviorist might consider applying all the SI products.

Product (Form) Psychologies

When we ask whether any school of psychology has featured products of information, we think naturally of Gestalt psychologists. In defining the concept of "product," I have said that it is the form that information takes, the way in which it is structured. This is also a good definition of a Gestalt. The basic distinction between content, as substance, and product, as form, is, of course, as old as Aristotle. It has cropped up in epistemologies in modern times, such as that of Kant.

Gestalt psychology came about from a realization that the third aspect of intellectual functioning had been seriously overlooked and that it is of considerable importance. The Gestaltists' polemics against elementarism and against the principle of association were incidental to their general rebellion. They were wrong to play down so severely the aspects of operations and contents, a case of "throwing out the baby with the bathwater," to use one of their favorite metaphors against them. But they were first to realize the importance of structured items of information, which are the SI products. In fact, they distinguished rather clearly most of those kinds of products. In harping on the primacy and the overriding importance of the totality of Gestalten, they were overdoing an emphasis. But for this they can be forgiven.

It would be unfair to say that the Gestalters paid no attention to operations. They did use the traditional concepts, such as perception, memory, and thinking, which dated back to faculty psychology. Had they aimed at the production of a comprehensive taxonomy, they should probably have given more attention to operations.

They did make a distinction between visual-figural and semantic content, without clearly labeling the latter, but they adopted the general principle that it does not matter with which kind of content the individual is dealing, the same principles of Gestalt apply. In their own investigations they were partial to visual-figural problems, by which they hoped to derive principles of more general application. Factor analysis has shown, however, that functioning *is* somewhat different for various kinds of content. But the fact that visual abilities are parallel with sets of abilities for other kinds of content in the SI model suggests that the Gestalters were partially right. At least some principles should apply to all kinds of content categories. But we should be alert to some that do not. Abilities differing in content are parallel, yes; identical, no.

Let us see how the SI products were approached in Gestalt thinking. In defining the product of "unit," I have often said that it is equivalent to the Gestalt conception of a "figure on a ground." But I should add that the emphasis should be on the figure. The term "figure" implies the SI visual-figural category, but as in Gestalt psychology, analogous phenomena are recognizable in different content areas.

In what sense are units of information structured, aside from the fact that they are differentiated from their backgrounds? In any content category, an SI unit is a segregated item of information, and it is a particular. It is structured by virtue of its having a unique set of attributes. A visual-figural unit has its properties of size, shape, color, texture, location, and orientation. A printed word, as a symbolic unit, has its unique combination of letters in a particular order. A meaningful conception of a boat, as a semantic unit, has its combination of features that identify it. A behavioral unit might be someone's intention to commit a hostile act—a unique state of mind.

Of all the SI products, systems most clearly fit the picture of a Gestalt, for they are clearly organized wholes—clearly structured items of information. A melody and a painting are examples of two different figural systems, one auditory and the other visual. But it takes different abilities to deal with the two. A list of nonsense syllables becomes a symbolic system, because of the temporal order involved. A verbally stated and conceived arithmetical problem is a semantic system. Three people interacting in a cartoon or in dramatic moment would provide a behavioral system. Two people interacting would provide a relation.

Of all the SI products, Gestalters emphasized most of all the roles of relations. They recognized classes, but made relatively little of them in constructing operational theories. On the other hand, they saw that relations play important roles in learning. This was partly incident to their efforts to find a replacement for the traditional concept of association. They delighted in showing that many events commonly called associations actually involve relations. There are numerous reports in Gestalt literature of the acquisition of new relations as keys to learning or problem solving (Helson, 1926). When the emergence of the new relation is sudden, it is said to involve an insight. Insight was thus frequently invoked as an explanatory step, and was presumably conceived as an act.

Many events of insight that Gestalters reported were of a different nature. These insights were reported to involve sudden shifts in Gestalten, shifts that were sometimes referred to as "redefinitions." In most cases, it is rather clear that they were reporting occurrences of the SI product of transformations.[4] They can surely be credited with being the first to recognize this kind of product. Having a transformation is a mental event that had been generally overlooked by other psychologists. Its relevance for creative thinking has been observed in recent years (Guilford, 1967). Except for a few isolated studies under the heading of insight or intuition, very little has been done to determine the conditions favorable for transformations and some of their consequences.[5]

The polemics of the Gestaltists against the securely entrenched principle of association makes an interesting chapter in the history of theoretical psychology. They were unable to show that every case of what is called an association involves a relation, but they did insist that a connection between two things psychological is dependent upon the properties of the things associated. Relations *are* dependent upon such properties.

Although they were very loath to accept the idea that an association can be formed fortuitously by the sheer fact of continguity of two things, they finally accepted association by contiguity as a limiting case, which yielded considerable polemic ground (Köhler, 1941; Wertheimer, 1945). What they needed is the SI distinction between relations and implications. They should have found very palatable the conception that in an association there is an implication; the one thing implies the other, a logical connection. It is thus not necessary to show that all associations are relations. Implications need not depend upon the properties of the things connected. The nature of the

---

[4]It is not clear whether Gestalters considered transformations as acts or as products of information. Logically, one can infer acts, but in the SI model, transformations have to be treated as products.

[5]Since recognition of transformations as an SI concept, investigations concerning it are beginning to appear (see Hoepfner, Guilford, & Bradley, 1970) (or Chapter 7 of this volume).

connection need not be specifiable. Thus, associations by contiguity attain respectable status as structured items of information, and can therefore be regarded as Gestalten. The Gestalters failed to note the product of implication, at least as a replacement for association.

Discussion

From the operational-informational view derived from the Structure-of-Intellect model, we can see that the historical points of view that have been concerned with intellectual functioning, in one way or another, have anticipated many of the SI concepts. Yet, each psychology has been very incomplete, in that it has tended to concentrate on one of the three dimensions of the SI model, to the neglect of others. There could have been considerably more progress under two conditions: the substitution of the concept of information for that of consciousness, and the recognition of the validity of inferential description.

Consciousness suggested sensory and feeling experiences to most of the pioneers, with no place for meanings—that is, semantic information—or other kinds of content. Information is a much broader concept, which includes not only the observed, figural information, but also other nonfigural varieties. The OI view might be taken to imply that not all information is conscious. Whether or not this is so, the occurrence of unconscious information can only be inferred rather than directly observed information. And this pertains to the second condition that should have helped: the recognition of the validity of inferential description.

Information is important in another way. The act psychologists cited the intimate connection between operations and information, but attempted to develop taxonomies without consideration of kinds of information. The functions indicated by the SI model are act-content-product affairs. A particular kind of function cannot be fully defined without considering three aspects, with its unique conjunction of operation, content, and product. As I have pointed out in some detail with respect to one operation category—memory—it is important in investigations to be aware of which of the twenty-four (or more) memory functions is involved (Guilford, 1971).

Other Theoretical Needs. To be complete, an OI psychology, or any view, must go beyond the realm of intellectual functioning. As should have been gathered from previous discussions, this particular view regards intellectual functioning as the processing of information of various substantive kinds under logical principles, where those principles are supplied by the products, the forms that information takes. A natural step toward a more complete psychology would be to see to what extent the SI concepts apply to other ranges of mental events.

Factor analyses outside the realm of intellectual functioning have not been so numerous, but there have been some, and bits and pieces of information are suggestive.

In one or more places (Guilford, 1965, 1973), I have advanced the thought that feelings and emotions, as well as aspects of motivation, could be regarded as behavioral information of the self-generated variety, as distinguished from behavioral information of the other-generated kind. This self-generated information gives us a running account of our personal states, of needs, of urgency, and of satisfactions, and so on. It is possible that at least some of the categories of informational products also apply. for example, such information comes in units; there are opposites, thus relations; one feeling leads to another, thus implications; and feelings undergo changes, thus transformations. A well-developed logic in this area would go a long way in generation of theory.

Theory regarding the motor side of behavior also stands to gain from discovery of unitary variables or functions and by development of taxonomies. I have shown how analyses of tests of rather simple nature yield psychological motor factors that can be organized in a morphological model in two dimensions, with categories such as impulsion, speed, coordination, and flexibility (Guilford, 1958).

Another type of psychomotor factor was forecast and was later demonstrated empirically (Hendricks, Guilford, & Hoepfner, 1969), in a general category called "executive functions." This type has to do with the organization and control of intended motor output. One factor was found for the production of vocal expressions of prescribed emotions, and the other for the production of facial expressions. I have put executive functions, in a genral model of behavior, in a sequence just preceding activation of selected muscles and just following intellectual functioning. These functions appear to provide the link between intellectual operations and motor discharges, something that is said to be a problem for cognitive psychology. It can be said by way of elaboration that the intellectual products of information have some isomorphism with the products of execution, so that one of the former can naturally lead to one of the latter.

This isomorphism implies, further, that executive functions have the same varieties of products as the intellectual functions. There appear to be units of directed motor action, classes of movement patterns, relations between movements, systems of movements, implications, and transformations. Except, possibly, for the operation of cognition, the SI operation categories also apply—memory, divergent production, evaluation, and, possibly, convergent production. The executive functions for producing emotional expressions are in the divergent-production category. They came out in an analysis that was primarily concerned with intellectual divergent production of behavioral information, but clearly separated from those intellectual functions (Hendricks, Guilford, & Hoepfner, 1969).

Summary

This presentation attempted to bring together and to extend some suggestions of how a comprehensive theory of a cognitive psychology could be based on the Structure-of-Intellect model as its basic taxonomy.

There was a consideration of historical systems or points of view in psychology, showing how each one tended to restrict itself very much to only one of the three aspects of the SI model. The structural, or existential, school limited itself to the content aspect of information, sometimes even to the category of figural (sensory) information. Act psychology attempted to get along with operation categories only, and did not distinguish many of those in the SI list. The "imageless-thought" psychologists were working in the direction of some of the SI operation and product categories. American functionalists stressed operations, using some ancient faculty-psychology concepts that have now been largely replaced by SI categories. Gestalt psychology was the only school that clearly recognized products of information, but neglected the other two aspects of the SI model. The school's informational concepts, of kinds of Gestalten, agreed with the SI products, except that Gestaltists failed to achieve the product of implication as a substitute for the concept of association, which they tried very hard to eliminate.

The proposed operational-informational psychology gives attention to all three aspects of the SI taxonomy. Suggestions were offered as to how the same concepts that apply to intellectual information processing can also be applied in the areas of motivation, emotion, and psychomotor activity. Further discoveries of factorial variables and functions in those areas should provide helpful taxonomies in which the SI concepts may be found to have extensive application.

Part II
Learning and
Memory

For almost any modern point of view in psychology there is high interest in problems of learning. Learning is broadly defined as any change in behavior that is due to behavior itself. Thus, accounting for learning is very much dependent upon the accounting for behavior itself.

Traditional theory of learning, from Ebbinghaus and E.L. Thorndike on, has rested on the foundation of associationism. This view now seems quite limited when compared with that derived from the SI model. The latter view goes in the direction of Gestalt theory, yet beyond it. It provides a solution to the problems that Gestalt psychologists raised regarding associations but never solved satisfactorily.

One of the most important ways that individuals learn in school and elsewhere is in the form of concepts. It has been demonstrated how the experimental application of factor analysis can yield useful information regarding this activity as well as the learning of psychomotor skills.

Investigation of the roles of the SI product of transformation in learning through reading has demonstrated the fact that much learning is actually relearning. Other indications point to the idea that much learning is reshaping of behavior that already exists.

Reinforcement—that important determiner of the persistence of changes—is interpreted in terms of the SI operation of evaluation. The general view is that an organism is a natural pragmatist. It cognizes what things work and what things do not, which is a matter of evaluation.

Textbook treatments of memory often discuss several steps: fixa-

tion, retention, and retrieval. Factor-analytic studies strongly indicate that only the first two steps apply to SI memory functions. It is
concerned only with putting items of information into memory storage. Retrieval of stored information is the important basis for two
different sets of SI functions: divergent production and convergent
production.

A full set of thirty memory abilities or functions envisaged by the
SI model parallels like numbers of functions of cognition, production,
and evaluation, for twenty of which there is empirical evidence. It is
imperative to pay attention to these varieties when considering experimental controls, as it has required such controls in order to
isolate them by factor analysis.

Chapter 5

An Emerging View

in Learning Theory[1]

Learning theory is very important, B. F. Skinner's assertions to the contrary (Skinner, 1950). Perhaps Skinner does not feel the need for learning theory because his research is rather limited to the implications of a single learning principle—reinforcement. Although reinforcement is a principle of first importance, most investigators recognize that there are other principles that also need investigation, and the various principles must somehow be brought into some degree of relationship. The basic investigator needs theory in order to help maintain his orientation toward his problems and subproblems. He also needs theory as a source of problems, as a means of judging their relative importance, and as a means of testing the significance of his hypotheses and his experimental findings.

The technologist who is concerned with education or training, particularly, also feels the need of learning theory. The history of modern education is to some extent an account of fads and fancies that have followed in the wake of changing theory, from Thorndike to the Gestalters to Freudians to Hull and Skinner. The increasing demands on education make attention to learning theory even more urgent. Lifelong education, involving education of the adult, seems to be an increasingly accepted responsibility of the schools. The changes in industry involving automation and the use of computers has an increasing impact on education as more technical skills are de-

---

[1]Largely extracted, with updating revisions, from Proceedings of the 1960 Summer Conference. Bellingham, Wash.: *Western Washington College Bulletin,* 1960, Pp. 29-46.

manded. The increased need for productive scientists and inventive engineers has helped to focus attention on the gifted student and has called for ways of accelerating progress and enriching educational offerings.

Shortcomings of Older Theories

New theory can often best be understood and evaluated against the backdrop of previous theory. At least there is some responsibility of the propounder of new theory to show where the older theory is inadequate. I shall attempt to do this in briefest terms.

Most of the orthodox theory in the past was based largely on research with rats and pigeons. Accordingly, there was little basis for psychological accounts of human learning, including comprehension, thinking, and problem solving. Often dominating the scene was the towering figure of Pavlov and his salivating dog. Without discounting the significant advances that the concept of conditioned responses has given to psychology, I am inclined to agree with Mowrer (1960) that classical conditioning is better restricted to the learning of autonomic responses. Some of the principles of conditioning apply by analogy to other areas of learning, but the case of their application becomes hopeless when this is carried so far as attempting to understand human problem solving.

Hull (1952) made a very admirable effort to work out all the logical implications of conditioning principles in behavior and added much to theory of learning and performance by giving attention to motivational aspects. Although his theory led to an enormous amount of research, I have a feeling that it took up much research time on problems of a less significant nature. There are other ways of interpreting the behavior phenomena that have been brought out by Hull's approach. They may not be as precise, but they have greater potential for generalizing.

Guthrie (1952) attempted to go all the way with the classical-conditioning model. More parsimoniously than others, he attempted to account for all learning on the basis of a single principle—contiguity. In general, I am suspicious of any theory that attempts to get along with only one concept. There is no denying that contiguity is a very important condition for learning. It is better regarded as a condition than as an explanatory principle. It is a favorable condition, but it is neither a necessary nor a sufficient condition.

It is possible to cite common instances in support of this statement. A person who thinks creatively commonly brings together two ideas (call them responses, if you wish) that he knows about but which have never been presented to him in contiguity. I am prepared to defend this act as an instance of learning, for the person has gained a connection that he did not have before. In this case, contiguity was not necessary. In general, if contiguity *were* necessary, we should be much more the victims of our environment than we are. Contiguity is not sufficient, for we are continually passing up opportunities for forming S-S or S-R connections, the conditions for which the environment is presenting us all the time. Guthrie was very ingenious in applying his contiguity principle, but his theory falls very short of success.

Seen in the perspective of history, Thorndike's principles of exercise and effect may be regarded as fair first approximations to descriptions of conditions of learning. We now know, however, that the effects of exercise are neither simple nor one-sided and that those results are a function of the interaction of exercise and effect. We also know that what Thorndike called "effect" and others call "reinforcement" is open to several different interpretations, and it is, indeed, not a simple condition. "Effect" appears to be a lasting concept, most theories taking it somehow into account.

Tolman (1949) has stood out as representing a quite different approach to learning theory; an approach that has sometimes been called "cognitive" theory. Although an avowed behaviorist, Tolman insisted that it is necessary to infer from observed situation and observed response of the learner. This runs counter to the general behavioristic dictum of staying very close to observed behavior. Although Tolman distinguished several kinds of learning, he did not follow through with a comprehensive or systematic survey of intervening processes. According to Miller, Galanter, and Pribram (1960), one of his serious failures was that he did not account for connections between cognitions and overt behavior.

Gestalt theory stimulated some very novel and refreshing observations of learning, and Gestalt psychologists made some very damaging criticisms of association theories, including the commonly favored stimulus-response models. There is much in Gestalt theory that is congenial to my own thinking, but the theory that will be proposed goes much further and provides many new concepts that are lacking in Gestalt psychology. The concept of insight is also given analytical meaning as well as empirical reference.

If you know something about my own background, you might expect me to be sympathetic to the learning theories that emphasize statistical models, such as those proposed by Estes (1950) and Bush and Mosteller (1955). Although this approach to theory must be admired, I am forced to recognize its limitations. There are certain types of research problems to which probability treatment seems most natural and fruitful. But there are other problems of behavior to which it does not apply so well. Another objection, which applies to most theories, is that they are confined to the stimulus-response model. We must break free from the bonds of such a limitation.

An Informational Psychology

I believe that the best way that we have at present for breaking away from the confines of a stimulus-response psychology is to be found through factor theory and the results of factor analysis. In particular, the analyses of intellectual abilities, leading to the production of the author's Structure-of-Intellect (SI) model (see Chapter 2, and particularly Figure 2.1).

The Importance of Information. Consideration of the categories into which the intellectual abilities have been catalogued shows that both the content and product categories pertain to information, its kinds of substance, and its forms. Of the total of sixteen categories, eleven pertain to information and five to operations. One could think of the content categories as being kinds of raw materials of information and the product categories as kinds of *manufactured* articles that the individual makes of the raw materials. Each product must be structured by the brain. I also think of the kinds of information—in a matrix of five columns for contents and six rows for products—as a systematic epistemology for psychology.

Association in the Structure of Intellect. Dating from Aristotle and the British empiricists, the principle of association has been a cornerstone of psychological theory, and has been the chief basis in accounting for learning. Only the Gestalt psychologists have seriously questioned that principle. It has, indeed, served psychology well, but I think that it must be superceded by more thorough-going concepts.

Of the concepts in connection with the Structure of Intellect, those that can most readily be given associative interpretations are the products of relations and implications. The other—units, classes, systems, and transformations—clearly have some totality properties that defy associative interpretations. Gestalters have also questioned whether a relation is adequately conceived as an association. Relations depend upon properties of the things connected in a relationship. When two things enter into a relationship, the relation is something more than an adhesive bond. A relation is a particular psychological event in its own right, just as any other product is.

Similar arguments could be stated regarding implications. The information that A leads to B or that C does not exist without D is more than a tie between the two in either case. It would appear that although the concept of "association" has served to apply loosely to a variety of phenomena, we can now do much better by specifying more clearly the nature of those phenomena.

An Informational Theory of Learning

An emphasis upon information and a discarding of the principle of association in favor of more analytical and more descriptive concepts takes us a long way toward a theory of learning. From this point of view, learning is a matter of acquisition of new items of information where acquisition means construction. Each item of information is unique; it differs from all other items. Thus, learning is also a matter of acquiring discriminations.

The Role of Products. As an example, let us take a favorite laboratory type of learning, the memorizing of a series of nonsense syllables. In SI terms, nonsense syllables are in the category of symbolic information. The memorizing of a list of syllables is in part a matter of getting acquainted with each and every item in the series. A memory for *units* is involved. This aspect of the task is often overlooked by investigators. In part it is a matter of discovering, or producing, and remembering *relations* between the items, with the help of properties that suggest relations. Lacking bases for relations, implications may be formed between successive pairs of items. Associative theory would recognize this type of event only. Syllables in a certain temporal sequence also constitute a symbolic *system*. This fact has been demonstrated in factor-analytic study of memory, and there is other evidence that can be cited for this conception of a series of items.[2]

And this isn't all. The resourceful learner, perhaps recognizing that memorizing semanic information is more efficient than memorizing symbolic items, may do some translating of his material into semantic form. He makes meaningful words out of some of the syllables, he verbalizes relationships, and he applies other semantic aids. In adopting such strategies in performing the learning task, the learner is programming himself, to use computer language. A strategy may be regarded as a system, probably semantic. The learner may have perviously learned such systems, or he may invent them to meet the circumstances. All this adds up to the fact that the act of memorizing simple-appearing material such as nonsense syllables may be very complex psychologically.

I can now explain an earlier statement regarding "insight," a term that has repelled many psychologists. One often noted feature of an insight is the unusual suddenness of learning or change. Probably all instances of the structuring of information take place in sudden steps, in quantum fashion. Steps can be large as well as small. The large, spectacular ones, gained attention and gave rise to the term "insight."

---

[2]For further evidence on this point, see Guilford, 1967.

Gestalt psychologists have frequently spelled out insight as the seeing of relations, but actually, from the informational view, an insight can be the emergence of any kind of product, from units to implications. There can be an empirical reference for an insight, for, as in Köhler's observation of the occurrence of insights in his apes, there are ways of inferring from overt behavior the fact that a certain insight has occurred.

The Role of Operations. Nothing particularly needs to be said regarding the roles of different kinds of content, except that it should be remembered that the abilities or functions involved in any learning event will also depend upon this aspect. We can gain much more useful information about learning by considering what roles the different SI operations play.

The roles of cognition and memory are obvious, since they account for the discovery (structuring) of new items of information and the committing of those items to storage. A thing is ordinarily not regarded as being learned unless there is some degree of retention beyond the moment of perception. Divergent production generates much new information in connections where it has never functioned before. Even convergent production can call forth resulting items that are novel to the learner at the time, as in achieving new deductions. Of all the operations, evaluation plays the most interesting and crucial role in what is commonly called "reinforcement."

It can probably be safely postulated that behavior is commonly self-corrective, at least potentially so. This principle has not been given sufficient attention by psychologists. It has been called to our attention by those who have developed the field of cybernetics. We cannot do many things without the guidance of feedback information. In standing erect, for example, we have a continual "balancing act" going on between excitations to the muscles involved and return messages, in a circular fashion. The same is true in reaching for an object or in driving a nail. For every muscular action there is an instantaneous report back and a correction, if necessary.

The self-checking and self-correcting feature of behavior applies also to intellectual processes, and this activity gives an important role for the SI operation of evaluation. In the general informational view, evaluation serves as the basis for reinforcement in learning. The concept of evaluation covers all the different interpretations of the concept of reinforcement. Clark Hull held that the key to reinforcement is drive reduction. An act that is followed closely by a lowering of need becomes established in response to the stimulating situation. The reduction of need is one kind of feedback information, and thus serves as one criterion of success. Thorndike's "confirming reaction" is very close in meaning to what I call evaluation. The feedback information confirms or fails to confirm whether or not the reaction just made is successful, suitable, or correct, or is otherwise a good one. Even when pleasure and pain are thought to be varieties of effect, they can be interpreted as feedback information, utilized by a learner in the operation of evaluation. The point is that the individual can use whatever feedback information he can get as an aid to evaluation of his actions. The learner is confirmed pragmatist.

Incidentally, the treatment of pleasure and pain as forms of information suggests that emotions generally may also be regarded as varieties of information. The appreciation of need reduction that was mentioned suggests that there is appreciation of the need itself, also in the category of information regarding motivation. Both emotional and motivational information are in the SI behavioral-content category. Such information gives the individual a running account of his internal states of well-being or ill-being.

Links Between Cognition and Action. Informational psychology comes under the general category of "cognitive psychology." The latter is sometimes criticized for lacking a good explanatory basis to account for the common linkage between perceived situations and motor reactions. The informational view can offer significant steps toward filling that gap.

All stimuli or situations, as perceived by an individual, imply potential action, which makes use of one of the SI products — implication. Whether or not a particular reaction is released in the presence of a particular situation will depend upon the individual's cognition of that situation and whether the action is cognized as suitable by the individual. We might think of the neural basis for an action as being a lock, as in a locked door. A certain key, or certain keys, will unlock the door; likewise the action. The point is that for a situation to instigate a certain motor response, there must be some kind of congruity or compatibility between the cognition of that situation and the action that is released, and such compatibility is also cognized.

It is possible to suggest things that may contribute to this compatibility. The individual has information concerning his own reacting mechanisms. He knows to some extent what they can and cannot do, and in what kinds of situations certain actions are suitable or effective. The properties of the objects that he cognizes, and their relationships and connections, call for movements with certain properties and perhaps for tools that can do certain things. The appropriate connections that the individual knows between objects and movements have been learned through innumerable trials and testings.[3]

A similar view has been proposed by Miller, Galanter, and Pribram, (1960). They speak of the "image" that the individual has of the world around him and of the "plan" that it suggests. Preceding any action there is a possible plan of action; a part of the individual's repertoire of plans. A plan is a hierarchical structure, having levels of strategies and tactics. In information psychology, a strategy is a system, which could be semantic or behavioral, or both. Such systems are built up through learning, for the most part. When action is called for, the individual indulges in matching his conceptions of plans and situations.

Transfer Effects. Historically, there has been considerable debate concerning whether effects of learning are general or specific, and, if general, how far the transfer extends. It is well known that the doctrine of formal discipline received some very hard blows from experimental findings, and there have been times when the extreme believers in specificity have fairly well dominated the scene. Factor theory and the knowledge of aptitude factors give us some new thoughts on these issues.

Woodworth and Schlossberg (1954) made the general statement that what is learned is an ability. Although the statement does not cover all cases, it is suggestive of the view proposed here. Multiple-factor theory, applied to the area of abilities, states that the total variance in measures of performance of a certain task can be attributed to several sources, some of which are common factors and one of which is specific. So long as the scores from a task correlate with scores from another task, the tasks concerned share at least one common factor. A typical task correlates at least with some other task, depending upon whether they have in common some necessary requirements. Most analyses show that each task has a specific component, peculiar to itself. Fleishman and Hempel (1954, 1955) have demonstrated in connection with more than one psychomotor task the fact that scores at different stages of practice reflect both common and specific factors. Furthermore, they were able to demonstrate some systematic changes in the importance of various factors as learning progressed.

Common factors possess some degree of generality and hence offer possibilities of transfer from one particular skill to another; the specific factor does not. Probably no task is completely general or

---

[3]For further elaboration of this discussion, see Chapter 3, which also brings into the picture the concept of "executive functions" as an additional link between cognized situation and motor response.

completely specific. There is thus a likely tieup between common factors and transfer. In fact, G. A. Ferguson (1954) recognized this fact and suggested that the common factors of ability develop as a consequence of transfer. It is generally recognized that where there is transfer, an important contributing condition for it is similarity of task. When we interpret and define a factor, it is in terms of the common psychological features that tests measuring the factor have in common. The tests for a certain intellectual factor are similar in three ways: in operation, in content, and in product. For tasks that are similar in all three ways, it should not be surprising that transfer will occur.

In Ferguson's view, each factorial ability is regarded as a unique kind of generalized skill. It develops as a consequence of exercise that involves as one of its components the same general skill. One implication is that in order to develop the intellects of children we must see to it that they have exercise in all the important SI abilities. It is probably too much to expect that each child shall achieve high levels in all respects, for heredity may well determine upper limits for individuals. How differential those limits may be is mostly unknown.

There are other questions regarding development. It may be that there are optimal times for development of different SI abilities at different ages. The order in which they naturally develop may be of importance, as the work of Piaget suggests. The maintenance of abilities through middle life and in the elderly years offers some problems. The roles of parents and teachers also need attention.

This line of thinking suggests that an important objective of education should again be to train the intellect. This implies formal discipline, but a new enlightened discipline.[4] It recognizes that exercise of one kind does by no means strengthen all of intellect, nor does it strengthen any faculty of very broad scope. There is transfer, indeed, but within limits.

Insofar as the SI factors themselves are interrelated, there are possible transfers beyond the scopes of those abilities. We have no good information as yet concerning correlations among the factors, but there are some indications of positive correlations, especially within product rows or content columns of the SI model. It seems reasonable to expect that if an individual becomes quite skilled in seeing relations in one kind of content there could be some transfer to seeing relations in other kinds of content. This would imply inter-correlations among the cognition-of-relations abilities. Much experience in dealing with behavioral information might have benefi-

---

[4]In this connection it is noteworthy that in Japan a Learned Society of Intelligence Education is promoting the use of exercise of SI functions, with emphasis at preschool and kindergarten levels. In the U.S.A. the *SOI* Institute is playing a similar role.

cial effects among behavioral abilities in general, preparing the individual to cope well with interpersonal relations. This would suggest positive correlations among many of the behavioral abilities (across product categories, for example). It is quite possible that if the individual knew about the nature of the SI model, with all its parallels, there would be much broader transfers in different directions.

Problem Solving and Creative Thinking

Problem solving and creative thinking can very well be included under the general heading of learning. There has been traditional recognition that problem solving often occurs in the process of learning. It can be regarded as an instance of learning, for when the person has solved his problem he has learned. He has information that he did not have before. A problem is a situation for which the individual has no ready, adequate response. His solution is a learned response. Problem solving involves creative thinking, for the solver must produce information that is novel, at least to him, which is characteristic of creative thinking.

In dealing with problem solving, psychologists have too generally fallen victim to the fallacy that one term means just one thing. Factor analysis has never demonstrated a unitary problem-solving ability that is common to all problem-solving tasks. As a matter of fact, items from different kinds of tests all present problems to the examinee if he does not immediately know the answers. There are actually many zero correlations among the different tests, all of which rather obviously present problems. This is the best empirical evidence against a belief in a unitary problem-solving ability.

Factor analyses of problem-solving tests have yielded abilities that belong somewhere in the Structure-of-Intellect model. One example of a factor-analytic study may be cited (Merrifield, Guilford, Christensen & Frick 1960). One major objective of the study was to determine whether a very general problem-solving ability could be found. Four tests were designed to more clearly call for problem solving because of their relative complexity. No such factor was found. Instead, these four tests were found to have significant relationships to the following abilities: CMU (cognition of semantic units), CMI (cognition of semantic implications), DMT (divergent production of semantic transformations), and EMI (evaluation of semantic implications). One could regard many other tests in the analysis also as problem-solving tests. Each of them was found to represent one or two SI abilities. These, and other findings, demonstrate just how heterogeneous problem-solving activities really are.

The factors found in any problem-solving test are functions of the intellectual resources it demands of the examinee and of the strategy he applies in its solution. Problems involving unusual degrees of ingenuity or creative thinking are likely to require sufficient status in divergent-production abilities and perhaps also in transformation abilities. There are numerous examples, one of which was a test called Planning Skills, which called for development of plans to meet a morale problem on a military base. Analysis (Berger, Guilford, & Christensen, 1957) showed that among the factors appreciably related to the scores from the test were DMT (divergent production of semantic transformations) and DMI (divergent production of semantic implications), both in the expected categories of factors.

These and other findings show that the factor-analytical approach can account for much of the variance in performances on complex problem-solving tasks. It should be remembered, of course, that the factor saturations in such a task apply to the group and not necessarily to any one individual. Each person may to some extent produce his own strategy, which may capitalize on his own points of strength and which may work around his points of weakness. But the information about how the average person of a certain population solves a kind of problem is of considerable interest, for it tells us much about the psychological demands of the task in question. This information should be basic to methods of instruction, and should tell us in what respects the task could contribute to intellectual development.

Summary

The purpose of this paper was to take steps toward the development of learning theory of a novel type, starting from factor theory, from known results of factor analysis, and from the concepts connected with the Structure of Intellect.

The kind of psychology suggested is called "informational" because the factors of intellect are so clearly differentiated along the lines of varieties of information. Learning is defined as a persisting change in behavior due to behavior. From the standpoint of the theory proposed, learning is the acquisition or structuring of new items of information.

In this theory, the principle of association is superceded by six kinds of products of information. An instance of learning may involve operations of cognition, memory, production (divergent or convergent), or evaluation, or any combination of these activities. Analyses of acts of problem solving of creative thinking bear out this statement. Evaluation is the key to reinforcement or effect, and logically it includes all common interpretations of those functions. In general, behavior is self-corrective, with built-in tests applied as activity proceeds. The link between cognition and motor action, in terms of informational theory, is, first, that cognitions imply motor responses, and, second, that there is appreciated congruency or compatibility between thoughts and actions, both in terms of information.

Chapter 6

Roles of Intellectual Abilities in the Learning of Concepts[1]

Concepts are ordinarily regarded psychologically as mental constructs, each pertaining to a set of objects, or events, based upon attributes that the set members have in common. I shall also refer to the same kind of construct as a class idea or class. In the repertoire of ·mental constructs that we possess, classes are among the most useful. They furnish taxonomies for stored information, and they play very important roles in retrieving information for use in problem solving and creative production. It is therefore very reasonable that an important objective of education should be concerned with the learning of concepts.

Efforts have been made, using various experimental procedures, to understand the processes involved in the learning of concepts. The effort reported here is a radically different one, using a multivariate approach to the analysis of individual differences in measurements of achievement in the learning of different kinds of concepts. Similar methods have been applied by Fleishman and others (Fleishman, 1966) to the analysis of learning scores in psychomotor tasks, with significant success. The procedures are sensitive and searching.

The Concept-Learning Tasks
Three parallel concept-learning tasks were used in the experiment, one for each of three informational content categories in the

---

[1]Reproduced, with minor editorial changes, from the *Proceedings of the National Academy of Sciences*, 1967, 58, 1812-1817. J. L. Dunham and R. Hoepfner were coauthors.

Structure-of-Intellect (SI) model. The materials in the three tasks provided the learner with three kinds of information—visual-figural (line drawings), symbolic (letters), and semantic (meaningful words). The reason for this duplication is that abilities in the SI model differ according to the kind of information being processed by the individual.

The exemplars for one of the visual concepts each contained a right angle, and those for another concept each contained intersecting lines. Each exemplar for a symbolic concept was composed of four adjacent capital letters, forming a nonsense word. The exemplars for one such concept each contained a repeated letter, and those for another each began with a vowel. An exemplar for a semantic concept was a set of four common words, one word of each set belonging to a certain meaningful class. In one case the words of the class stood for kinds of leaders, and in another case the words indicated sounds made by animals.

Each task was in the category of concept discovery, in which the experimental subject *(S)* is presented with exemplars of a class one at a time, and he attempts to achieve the correct understanding of the concept. Since four concepts were involved in each task, the exemplars belonging to each class were presented in mixed, random sequence. There were twenty-four exemplars for each concept, making ninety-six presentations in each task. Each presentation was made on a separate page of a "teaching book." In group administration of the tasks the *S*s were signaled to turn a page every five seconds. Before finishing with the page, *S* was to encircle one of the four letters, A, B, C, or D, with which he also had to learn to associate the four concepts, respectively. On turning a page, *S* found the preceding exemplar repeated along with its correct letter for the class to which it belonged. *S* was thus provided with immediate feedback information regarding the right and wrong answers. The three tasks were administered on three different days.

The major objective of this investigation was to determine the extent to which scores made by individuals in the learning tasks are related to selected intellectual abilities that are represented in the SI model. Any measure of performance in trials during practice on the learning task (except for the very first trials) should reflect the effects of practice. Another objective was to determine whether the relative importance of certain abilities changes systematically with practice. Accordingly, learning scores were obtained. Each stage score was the number of correct answers from eight successive trials, which gave twelve stage scores for each individual in each task. The means of the stage scores from the 177 *S*s ranged approximately from 4 to 7, which means that all the stage-score means were above the chance level and below the ceiling level of 8.0, thus providing room for usable variance in individual differences, an important condition for success with the multivariate approach.

The Abilities and Their Tests

Of all the abilities either known or hypothesized in the SI model, the ones concerned with classes of items of information seemed logically most relevant as resources in connection with the learning of concepts. Fifteen of these were of interest in this study, since they pertained to the three kinds of content involved. Three cognition-of-classes abilities are concerned with the mere knowing of class ideas, as when S is presented with a set of members of a class and he recognizes what class idea is involved. Three memory-for-classes abilities are involved in tests in which S can show that he has not only observed but has stored class ideas in memory. The divergent-production abilities involve acts of classifying *and reclassifying* a group of objects, where alternative groupings are possible. The three convergent-production abilities apply where there is only one basis for classification; the groups are unique and mutually exclusive. A possible fifth set of evaluation abilities was not represented by tests in this study due to lack of testing time with the subjects. One memory-for-classes ability, that for visual information, was not included for lack of available tests. It had not yet been investigated by factor analysis.

Four abilities outside the classes category were represented by tests, but they are of little interest in this limited report. From scores earned by the Ss on forty-three tests for fifteen abilities, a factor analysis was performed in order to establish a factor structure to be used as a frame of reference, each factor being represented by an orthogonal dimension. From known correlations between the learning-stage scores and the factor-test scores, the vectors representing those learning variables were later located within the factor reference frame. Factor loadings were determined for the learning scores indicating degrees of relationship to all fifteen abilities.

Relations of Learning Scores to Factors

The factor loadings for the learning scores were almost all on the positive side, reflecting the fact that the SI abilities generally made positive contributions to the learning of the concepts. This result also means that many of the correlations are not merely chance deviations from zero. Unfortunately there are no known ways for estimating statistical significance of factor loadings.

The communalities of the twelve stage scores ranged from 0.11 to 0.39 in the visual task, 0.10 to 0.31 in the symbolic task, and 0.12 to 0.48 in the semantic task. Such proportions of the variances of the learning scores could thus be regarded as accounted for by the class abilities included in this study. The reliability estimates for the learning scores were higher than these values, however, indicating that some of the variance that could be accounted for was not accounted for. Some of this surplus variance might represent SI abilities not included in this analysis.

In general, the higher the factor loading in a learning score the more involved is the particular ability in contributing to individual differences in that score. On the other hand, a loading of zero would not necessarily mean that an ability is not involved in a task. It merely indicates that individual *differences* in the ability do not contribute to individual differences in performance. For a *trend* in factor loadings to appear, many individuals in a group of *S*s must synchronize their emphases upon a factor, stressing it more at one stage than at another. Such emphases would depend upon the strategies of the *S*s in their learning task.

There were a number of observable trends in the relations of factor loadings to ability as functions of practice. The nature of these trends was more clearly shown after smoothing, by application of the method of running averages to the data points. Concerning the relations of abilities to learning only in cases where the content category is the same in task and test (visual abilities and visual task, and so on), definite trends can be seen in eight of eleven instances. The other three cases showed essentially uniform loadings over all stages of practice. Four examples of the more definite trends are shown in Figures 6.1 and 6.2.

In six of the cases showing trends, the loadings varied from very low at the beginning of practice to relatively high at the end. In two of these cases, the abilities were represented by *negative* loadings in the earliest stages, with loadings crossing the zero level later in the learning event (see Figure 6.1). The negative loadings should mean that those two abilities were handicaps near the beginning but later became helpful contributors to performance. The two abilities were in the category of cognition, which may mean that a too facile recognition of possible class ideas causes trouble until corrective information has accumulated in a series of trials. In the parallel third case (not shown), of regression for the ability of cognition of visual classes on practice in the visual task, there was an early rise in loading, starting at about the zero level, with some decline setting in beyond the midpoint of practice and continuing to the end. One other relationship among the eleven trends was of this type.

Of the four SI operation categories involved in this study, that of memory abilities appeared to make the greatest contribution to learning (see Figure 6.2). This fact is probably due to the method of presenting the exemplars one by one, which made it necessary for *S* to

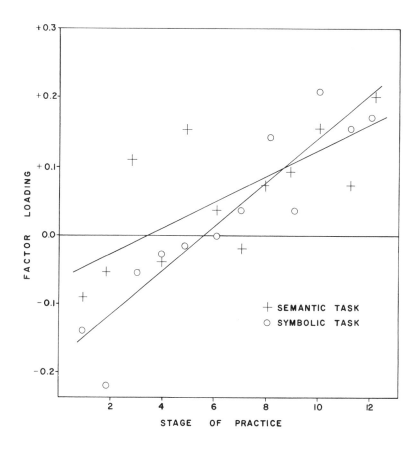

6.1. *Linear regressions of factor loadings for two cognition abilities as functions of practice on two tasks. (The linear correlations were .73 and .93, both significant beyond the .01 level.)*

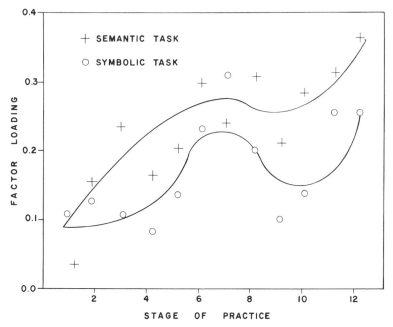

6.2 *Nonlinear relationships between factor loadings for the ability of memory for semantic and symbolic classes and stages of practice. (The nonlinear correlations were .88 and .86, both significant beyond the .01 level.)*

remember classes from trial to trial. It will be noted that in Fig. 6.2 the regressions are not linear. There were systematic drops in relative importance of memory, for semantic classes especially, about three-fourths of the way in practice. The overall positive contribution of this ability is indicated by the fact that nine of its twelve loadings were greater than 0.20 for the semantic task. But it also had five loadings of similar size for the symbolic task, and three for the visual task. These semantic-ability loadings in nonsemantic tasks suggest that the *S*s tended to conceive of the classes in semantic form and were remembering them in that language regardless of the form in which the exemplars were presented. Meaningful or semantic information is more readily remembered than other kinds, and it is often found in experiments that employ visual or symbolic information that *S*s sometimes translate such information into more readily remembered form. But in this experiment, there were some signs of translation in other directions as well. A human subject is a very resourceful creature at times.

The divergent-production abilities appeared to contribute least to the total variance of learning scores. This is understandable in that producing alternative classifications was not the obvious feature of the tasks. Eventually, S was to arrive at four unique classes in each task, hence we should expect more of a role for convergent production, particularly toward the end of practice. Along the way, however, some substitutions of class ideas were no doubt needed, and this is where divergent-production abilities could play roles. Loadings for the divergent-production abilities were systematically on the positive side, although very small.

Conclusions

In conclusion we see that the learning of concepts, in the form utilized in this study, at least, is a very complex affair, drawing upon many different abilities or functions. It is best to conceive of such an event as an episode of problem solving in which the individual brings to bear whatever resources seem promising. Different individuals agree well enough on which resources are utilized at different stages of learning to produce the kinds of trends in factor loadings that were mentioned.

The implications of these findings for education are numerous. For one thing, we see the importance of SI abilities for dealing with classes. It is a remarkable fact that such abilities have heretofore been entirely absent from standard intelligence scales and also of little consideration in experiments on concept learning. Knowing which abilities are relevant to a certain kind of learning task, we are better able to instruct a learner as to what basic operations are involved and at what learning stage, and we can warn him of potential difficulties, particularly near the beginning of the learning event. Being able to give this kind of information quite generally, of course, implies numerous prior studies of this kind, both for different kinds of concepts and concept-learning events and for different age groups and educational levels of subjects.

Chapter 7

Transformation of Information

in Learning[1]

The objective of this study was to determine the extent to which intellectual abilities for dealing with transformations are related to learning in academic subjects. In the Structure-of-Intellect (SI) model, transformation abilities are those concerned with changes of various kinds—revisions, rearrangements, substitutions, redefinitions, and the like.

Some Known and Expected Relations

The unique role of transformations in intellectual functioning is suggested most readily by their relation to flexibility in problem solving and creative thinking, both of which may occur in acts of learning. Learning is best simply defined as change in behavior consequent to behavior itself. Thus, it is possible that learning involves transformations of information; initial cognitions give way to new ones, and new ones come by way of revisions of old ones. "Transformation" is a change concept and so is learning.

It is common knowledge that traditional aptitude tests do a fair job of predicting status at the end of learning, but they leave something to be desired. This probably means that something about achievement in learning is left unaccounted for that could be accounted for, and that this something is in the area of transformation abilities. There is some scattered evidence that this is true (Cline, Richards, & Abe, 1962; Getzels & Jackson, 1962).

---

[1]Adapted by permission, with a few minor changes, from the *Journal of Educational Psychology,* 1970, 61, 316-323. R. Hoepfner and P. A. Bradley were coauthors.

Kluever (1968) found significant differences between groups of thirty normal readers and thirty disabled readers in the fourth grade in memory tests for both symbolic and semantic transformations, abilities MST and MMT, particularly. Kluever also found that the MMT score correlated significantly with a standard achievement test score for reading comprehension, for students with reading disabilities. In a multiple-discriminant function for distinguishing normal and disabled readers, the MST score was the best discriminator and the MMT score was the second best when the discriminant function involved memory scores only. When achievement variables and IQ subscores were included in the discriminant function, MST still entered the function, second in weight only to overall achievement level in reading—the variable on which the two groups were formed.

By inspection, examples of the roles of transformations in various courses are easy to find. In mathematics, the student who factors algebraic expressions or solves equations is dealing with symbolic transformations. The budding scientist who revises his hypotheses as he is confronted with new information is also involved with transformations. In the arts and in creative writing, transformations are the order of the day. At any place in the educational scheme where the purpose is the assimilation of information with the goal of seeing new and different applications or the solving of problems based on the given information, transformation abilities should be involved.

The overriding characteristic of academic learning is the comprehension of information obtained through reading and its retention to meet future needs. It is also true that a task that demands the recall and use of the information is likely to be different from the one in which the information was originally cognized. Since education is based upon the premise that learned information may be generalized or transferred to new problem situations, academic learning is often subjected to different conditions for mental "input" and "output." Learning that involves transformations would seem to provide an optimal circumstance.

Measuring School Learning

School learning is defined for this study as the acquisition of information by reading. Grade points or grade-point averages, also scores from course examinations, were rejected as criteria as being too complex psychologically, hence ambiguous, and as having irrelevant content. The criterion of school learning that was used was based upon a specially designed task; a reading-comprehension test, but not an ordinary one. In the student's typical learning situation he studies the information to be learned and is examined on it in some way some time later, with the reading material removed. The criterion test was designed to duplicate this series of activities, except that the quizzing occurred immediately after reading. There could still be a significant amount of memory variance involved in the scores, so there was interest in abilities for memory for transformations. There would also be the possibility of variances in cognition and evaluation of transformations.

In order to control for some other variances in the learning task, the reading material was selected and the multiple-choice test items were constructed so that words would be relatively familiar. This step was designed to minimize variance in CMU—cognition of semantic units, or verbal comprehension—which usually dominates ordinary reading-comprehension tests. In order to control for variance in previous knowledge, the reading content was composed of subject matter that was relatively novel to the students. In order to ensure reasonable interest in the material, the topics were (1) protein and starvation; (2) psychedelic drugs; and (3) stockmarket trends. The material also dealt with lesser known aspects of these subjects.

Each section of the learning test was composed of two parts. The first part allowed four minutes to a study page on which was an essay of about 400 words. The material was designed to present a maximum amount of information per unit of time. The second part of a section was a test page on which the subject was to answer ten items. The items were all of a factual nature, none being of the application or inference type. On the basis of a prior item analysis, those items were retained that were answered significantly more often by Ss who had read the material than by those who had not. Test scores would thus depend less upon long-term memory stores and more on shorter-term memory of newly studied information. The scores from the three parts were summed for each student to obtain a more representative and reliable estimate of his school-learning performance.

The Transformation Abilities and Others

The subjects were also administered a large battery of tests for a factor analysis that was focused on transformation abilities. The battery included tests for ten transformation abilities plus tests for a few other SI abilities. The transformation abilities were concerned with semantic and symbolic content and involved all five SI operations. These ten transformation abilities are described below (with reference to characteristic tests):

CST—cognition of symbolic transformations—is the ability to recognize that certain symbolic transformations have occurred. Tests for it require S to see that there have been changes in spelling, in anagrams, or in other units or systems.

CMT—cognition of semantic transformations—involves seeing

changes in meaning or the interpretation of things. Understanding a pun is one example.

MST—memory for symbolic transformations—involves remembering changes in letter or number material. In one test, S studies a list of misspelled familiar words and is later given a list of correctly spelled words to which he is to respond with the transformed words that he had seen.

MMT—memory for semantic transformations—can be tested by giving S puns or homonyms. A test follows to determine how well he remembers the changes, as such.

DST—divergent production of symbolic transformations—is concerned with the production of various, alternative changes in material such as that composed of letters or words. A test of DST is open ended. Starting with the same item of information, S is to suggest a number of different ways of changing it, following certain general rules.

DMT—divergent production of semantic transformations—is measured by having S suggest alternative meaningful responses to a starting idea, all of which involve changes, as in producing alternative puns, or clever titles for a story.

NST—convergent production of symbolic transformations—can be tested by asking S to make new words out of given ones following certain specified requirements that would lead to another particular word.

NMT—convergent production of semantic transformations—is represented by tests that call for particular new uses for familiar objects or parts of objects, like using a tablecloth to make a distress signal.

EST—evaluation of symbolic transformations—may be tested by asking S to say whether given anagramatic changes have been properly done.

EMT—evaluation of semantic transformations—would be involved in tasks asking S to say whether unusual adaptations of objects are clever or adequate.

The six additional SI abilities that were covered in the factor analysis and that could also be studied in relation to the learning criterion include the following:

CSU—cognition of symbolic units—is shown by recognition of printed words as letter combinations, for example. Test items might be anagrams, or words with vowels missing to make the items sufficiently difficult for testing purposes.

CMU—cognition of semantic units—is understanding of word meanings, best tested by vocabularly tests.

CMI—cognition of semantic implications—is an ability to see

associated items of information, as in predicting or forecasting.
MSI—memory for symbolic implications—is the ability to remember arbitrary connections between symbolic items of information, as in paired-associate memory experiments.
DSI—divergent production of symbolic implications—would be
featured in a task in which S is to derive several different equations
from two given equations that have some elements in common.
DMC—divergent production of semantic classes—is represented in
tests in which, given the name of a familiar object, S is to supply
different classes in which it is a member, or, given a list of words, he
is to group and regroup them in different classes.

It was not expected that all the sixteen abilities would be related to
the learning criterion. To some extent, then, the study was in the
nature of a "fishing expedition." As stated at the beginning, the major
interest was in the transformation abilities, and some of *them* might
not be expected to have significant relationships.

Procedures
The subjects for this study were 197 students in a middle-class high
school in Los Angeles. They were in a "gifted" program, so were
presumably a highly talented group. The sample comprised 100
males and 97 females, of whom 77 were sophomores, 78 were juniors,
and 42 were seniors.

Instead of examining the relations of learning scores to each of the
forty-seven tests in the battery, following the factor analysis, sixteen
factor scores for each of the Ss were estimated by Bartlett's (1937)
method. It was believed that this approach yields clearer conclusions
regarding the relevance of each ability for the learning performance.
Examination of the intercorrelations among the 16 factor scores
found them to be all near zero (the factors were orthogonal).[2] The
situtation was thus ideal for multiple regression analysis.

The analysis was carried out in step-wise fashion, in which the
predictor variables are added to the equation in the order of their
strength of contribution and the addition of variables is stopped when
any regression coefficient becomes statistically insignificant.

Table 7.1 presents the regression equations with the significant
beta weights of the factor scores for predicting the learning scores.
This table also presents the multiple-correlation coefficients in three
samples. The first equation presents the statistics for the whole group
of students, with a multiple R of .58. The second and third equations
present similar statistics for two randomly selected samples from the

---

[2]Only 10 percent of the intercorrelations were greater than .10 in either direction,
the range being from $-.14$ to $+.13$.

Table 7.1   Statistics for Three Regression Equations

Sample Equations, with Beta Weights		Multiple R	Cross-Validated R	N
Total .40 CMU	+.32MMT +.22CMT +.20DST +.16EST +.16DMC +.14NMT	.58	—	197
A	.40CMU +.23DMC +.23MMT	.48	.43	99
B	.40CMU +.37MMT +.30CMT +.27DST +.23EST +.17NMT	.67	.42	98

All statistics significant at the .01 level except for the betas for NMT, which were significant at the .05 level.

total group. The resulting multiple Rs for these two groups were .48 and .67. A double-cross-validation procedure, employing the regression weights derived from the one sample to predicting learning scores in the other subsample yielded correlations of .43 and .42, respectively.

Factor Involvements in Learning[2]
To the extent that the criterion of school learning used in this study represents that kind of activity generally, we can make some statements regarding certain factorial contributions to success in that activity. Not unexpectedly, the CMU factor, verbal comprehension, appeared as the leading contributor to learning performance in two of the equations and was in second place in the third. This was in spite of the fact that, as mentioned earlier, efforts were made to minimize the effect of that ability. Had the reading material contained more unfamiliar terms, the relation of CMU should have been greater.

The second strongest contributor, with a beta weight not far behind that for CMU in the total sample, was the score for MMT, or memory for semantic transformations. This suggests that the subjects cognized transformations in reading the test essays, and they were stored sufficiently in memory to function while taking the following multiple-choice test. It can thus be hypothesized that S sees or produces changes in his previously held information as he reads the material, or as he rechecks his information while he reads. His retention of transformations may even help him to recall units of information that were involved.

---

[2]Where an SI-ability trigram is given without the name spelled out here, a quick reference can be made to preceding pages. In general, reference can be made to the Appendix, where a complete code is given relating trigram and name of ability.

Because MMT was found to be significantly related we should expect CMT also to be in that category, for things remembered must be first cognized. CMT was significantly related in two of the prediction equations. A hypothesis that S sees transformations perhaps for the first time during his answering the test items cannot be ruled out. For example, his reading of the alternative answers to an item may suggest to him that he was wrong about some point during his reading. Seeing such changes should also involve CMT.

Although the two parallel abilities, CST and MST, which could have been expected to have some relevance in the learning task, did not prove to be significantly related, the "fishing expedition" did suggest a few other findings of interest, two of them involving symbolic information. They were DST and EST, both in two regression equations. The symbolic involvement can possibly be attributed to the fact that two of the three reading selections included numerical material. The relevance of divergent production and evaluation operations suggests the hypothesis that some trial-and-error behavior was going on, probably during the taking of the memory test. It is suggested that some guessing was going on concerning the numerical values (DST) and self-checking regarding the guesses (EST).

The involvement of DMC in the learning test as shown by two of the equations can be rationalized. This result suggests that the Ss were engaging in the production of alternative class ideas, either during the reading or during the memory test, or both. Developing new understanding puts ideas in new classes. It is possible that while reading the paragraphs S finds that he has to reclassify some old ideas. It is also possible that during the memory test some alternative answers suggest the need for new classifications. In either case there would be a need for flexibility of classes.

Ability NMT, also involved in two of the equations, is concerned with deducing logically necessary conclusions from given information, where the conclusions are transformations or they result in transformed items of information. It may be that S remembers enough facts from his reading so that when a particular fact is demanded by the memory-test item, some other fact, properly revised, will point to the needed answer. It is sometimes recognized by teachers that students may select a right answer "by reasoning" rather than from memory. The "reasoning" may well involve some kind of transformation.

An important general point is that, of all the abilities here demonstrated as being relevant to school learning, only one—CMU—is known to be covered by common academic-aptitude tests. Also of general interest is the fact that so many transformation abilities are relevant. It is true, of course, that the selection of abilities to be investigated in the study was biased toward transformations. It is sometimes found that CMS, for example, is relevant in reading-comprehension tests, and it was not included. At any rate, the relevance of transformation abilities has been demonstrated.

It may be of psychological importance that among other abilities not contributing to significant predictions are some concerned with implications—CMI, MSI, and DSI. This is especially interesting because implications abilities are clearly concerned with what have been traditionally known as "associations," or associative connections. These three abilities are concerned with associations—seeing associations, memory for associations, and production of associations, respectively—yet none of these activities showed up in terms of individual differences. In this connection it must be admitted that the multiple-choice test items were not written in such a way that paired-associate learning and memory were directly involved. Neither would it be fair to conclude that other implications abilities, such as MMI, would not be found relevant, had they been included.

Discussion

The finding that seven of the sixteen aptitude factors investigated in this study have significant relationships with the measure of school learning, demonstrates quite clearly the shortcomings of commonly utilized educational prognostic instruments. From this finding we see some interesting possibilities for improving prediction of learning achievement. The exploration could be extended to still other SI abilities. Speculatively, it might be suggested that some promising candidates for investigation in this connection might be SI abilities CMS, MMU, MMS, MMI, EMU, and EMI.

Summary

A studying-and-remembering task, designed to simulate typical academic learning, was utilized in a test of academic achievement. From forty-seven tests, composite scores were derived to measure sixteen Structure-of-Intellect abilities, ten of them being in the category concerned with the SI product of transformations, in the content areas of semantic and symbolic information, and in all five operation categories.

Regression analysis showed that five of the ten transformation abilities had statistically significant weight, as did two of the other six abilities represented in this study. One of the latter was CMU (verbal comprehension), which usually dominates reading-comprehension tests. Reading and remembering are thus very complex activities in their demands on intellectual resources. The study also illustrates how other complex activities can be described in terms of intellectual requirements.

Chapter 8

Varieties of Memory
and Their Implications[1]

The increase in numbers of publications on memory indicates a considerable growth of interest in that subject. There are also signs of growing sophistication in approaches and methods. In large part these advances can be attributed to the freeing of investigators from the highly restrictive views of stimulus-response theory and to innovative substitutions of informational thinking in psychology. But too many investigators are still working within the confines of an associational frame of reference when a new and more comprehensive view is needed.

It is the primary purpose of this paper to point out some implications derived from research on memory in the Aptitudes Research Project (ARP) at the University of Southern California, for the findings from that source have much to offer by way of new understandings of the nature of human memory. Those findings provide a comprehensive, systematic taxonomy of distinguishable memory functions that has not been available before. The taxonomy yields new concepts to serve as handles by which to lay hold of problems, to provide interpretations of results, and in general to serve as a frame of reference.

The need for such concepts can best be appreciated by consideration of some inadequacies of traditional distinctions. It has been common practice to speak of rote memory versus meaningful memory versus logical memory, and of verbal memory versus nonverbal memory.

[1]Adapted with permission from the *Journal of General Psychology,* 1971, 85. 207-228.

These qualifying terms applied to memory have very rarely been rigorously or unambiguously defined. It will be shown how these concepts can be replaced with others that are more precisely defined and that also have clear empirical referents.

The availability of such new concepts calls for some needed refinements in research operations. The concepts should function in the planning of research because the distinctions that they make point to variables that should be taken into account, and experimental controls that are needed. Experiences incident to the discovery of these concepts have revealed the needs for such controls.

Evidence will be presented for the distinctions made among the taxonomic categories of memory, and examples of definitive tests will be given. The tasks and materials in these tests are the empirical referents for the different memory functions. The properties of the tasks point not only to the nature of the functions concerned, but also to the taxonomic categories of the functions and to some of the experimental controls needed in their investigation.

Memory in the Structure of Intellect

In the Structure-of-Intellect (SI) model, memory is recognized as one of the five basic kinds of intellectual operations of which human individuals are capable.[2] Intellectual functioning is a matter of processing information according to logical principles. This definition will be explained later. Information is defined as that which the individual discriminates. It is in the form of items, each unique. Among the events intervening between stimulus input and motor output, the operation of cognition (including perception), which is a matter of encoding information in various forms that represent environmental features, is naturally first. Some of the encoded information is fixated or committed to memory storage. Thus, the operation of memory must be distinguished from the memory store. The kinds of evidence that are used to show that certain items of information have been stored, and to what degree, are well known. The information may be retrieved for use in various connections, some of which have not been previously learned, as shown in productive operations, divergent or convergent. In SI conceptions, retrieval of information from storage is not a memory function; it is an operation of production. Realizing this may help to clarify matters.

The Memory Matrix. As for the other basic operations in the SI model, the memory category includes thirty distinct memory functions, as shown in Table 8.1.[3] There are thirty such functions because there

---

[2]For a description of the SI model, see Chapter 2.
[3]In accordance with the latest version of the SI model (Guilford, 1977a).

Table 8.1   A Matrix of Memory Abilities or Functions
from the Structure of Intellect

Visual (V)	Auditory (A)	Symbolic (S)	Semantic (M)	Behavioral (B)	
MVU	MAU	MSU	MMU	mbu	(U) Units
MVC	mac	MSC	MMC	mbc	(C) Classes
MVR	mar	MSR	MMR	mbr	(R) Relations
MVS	MAS	MSS	MMS	mbs	(S) Systems
MVT	mat	MST	MMT	mbt	(T) Transformations
MVI	mai	MSI	MMI	mbi	(I) Implications

are thirty unique kinds of information. The latter constitute what the writer has proposed as a psycho-epistemology. They arise from the fact that there are five kinds of informational content and six kinds of informational products. Each memory function is labeled with a trigram symbol, in capital letters if it has been demonstrated by factor analysis, in lower-case letters if not.

SI Memory and Memory Tests

Further light on the conception of memory as a Structure-of-Intellect category (and of its many varieties) can be obtained from a consideration of the kinds of tests by which the memory functions have been differentiated. Memory tests present the test developer with special difficulties, and some of the special test forms raise interesting questions in relation to kinds of memory functions. Let us consider some of the gross features first.

Many memory tests have had their counterparts in the experimental laboratory, but most are in novel forms unknown in that context. For example, some are variants of such tasks as those for memory span, serial memorizing, and paired-associates learning. Some of the more superficial differences between tests used for factor analysis and those of the laboratory are incident to group testing versus individual testing. In a factor-analytic study, where some fifty tests are administered to some 200 subjects or examinees (*S*s), individual testing is prohibitive. This means that in some tests there is some loss of control of the time that S devotes to each presented item. Exceptions are for visual material projected on a screen or tape-recorded sound material.

In most cases the practice has been to present the items to be memorized with limited time on a "study page." It is not known how much loss there may be in terms of reliability and validity by this procedure. At any rate, estimates of reliability and of (factorial) validity are routinely obtained in a factor-analytic experiment, whereas they are rarely or never known in a bivariate laboratory experiment.

On the other side of the picture, there has been some effort in the factor-analytic approach to exert controls that are rarely applied in the psychological laboratory. First, there has been concern for controlling differential effects of other kinds of SI operations while investigating the operation of memory. More specifically, there has been concern for keeping individual scores free of any unacceptable contributions from individual differences in the other operations— cognition, production, and evaluation.

A crucial way in which memory tests differ from tests of other operational functions, is, of course, in their two-stage feature. That is, there must be a memorizing event followed by a testing event. In the first of the two events, the material must be of such a nature that it can be fully cognized by S, lest cognitive variance be introduced. Just to be at ease on this point, it has been common to include in the analysis some marker tests for cognition abilities that are parallel to memory abilities under investigation. In this way it can be determined whether cognition variance has been adequately controlled. Sometimes it is not, but this fact can become known from results of the analysis.

Because many of the memory tests require *recall* of the items to be memorized, and because the operations of divergent and convergent production are so dependent upon retrieval of information from the memory store, it might be expected that recall tests, in contrast with recognition tests, would show correlation with production tests, and that either production tests would have some memory variance or memory tests would have some production variance. There is a logical distinction that should call for reservations, however, and that is concerned with the original sources of the stored information. The information to be retrieved in memory tests has been stored under recent, controlled conditions, whereas that for the production tests was stored without special controls, in different contexts, and is of longer, mixed duration. But to check on this question, marker tests for production abilities, mostly divergent, were sometimes included in analyses of memory abilities. The outcome has been so decisive that even with recall-memory tests there are near-zero correlations with production tests, with rare exceptions.

Within the memory domain, there has been concern about differentiating functions that differ with respect to kinds of content and kinds of products. In accordance with experiences in other operational areas, there has been more concern about differentiating abilities differing in products than those differing in content. Abilities for different content categories have usually been easier to segregate. In either case, differentiation is dependent upon the effectiveness of experimental controls that are built into the tests. But in the memory area, because of the two-stage nature of the tests, good control is not so easy to achieve. *S*s can more readily invent and apply their own strategies, which may circumvent the carrying out of the investigator's intentions.

In the studies in which I was involved, there were few instances in which parallel memory abilities differing only in content were investigated in the same analysis. But it must be recognized that the five kinds of content are like different languages, and there are possibilities for *S* to encode the information in a language not intended or to recode the information in a second language some time before he answers the test items.

Miscarriages of encoding as to products are expected to be more common during the stage of memorizing. For example, where only an implication was intended within a pair of items, such as words, *S* sees a relation and remembers the connection as such. This kind of substitution has been implicitly recognized at times in laboratory studies. A factor analysis can show that it has happened, and to what extent, by a loading of the memory-for-implications test on the memory-for-relations factor. Sometimes in a figural-relations item such as a large square paired with a small square with a relation of size, *S* sees it as a shrinking, which is a transformation. An accumulation of such substitutions shows up in terms of a memory-for-transformations factor in a memory-for-relations test. Incidentally, factor analysts who favor oblique rotations of axes would probably take such results to indicate correlations between factors. My view, however, is that we should consider possible failures of controls before we entertain that hypothesis.

Some further comments regarding the special nature of the factor-analyzed tests that were used in the ARP studies are relevant here. The retention interval was rather short, but hardly so short as to put the tests in the short-term (STM) category. In saying this, the writer adopts the common conception that STM involves functional retention over a very few seconds. In the analyzed tests, an interval of about two minutes was typically allowed for *S* to study the material to be memorized. He was then told to turn the page and begin work on the retention test. Thus, the retention interval for different items in that material ranged from the page-turning time to two minutes or more. It was thought that long-term memory functions were being investigated, indirectly if not directly, since the quantity of retained information that could be detected after a lapse of a week or longer should be dependent upon what can be evidenced within the first five minutes, barring reminiscence effects.[4]

It should be mentioned that in the ARP research both recognition and recall tests were designed for every expected factorial ability. This was done in order to determine whether distinctions would be forthcoming between possible recognition and recall functions. No such distinctions were realized, but it can be said that the correlations within recognition tests and within recall tests for the same factor were a bit higher than those between the two kinds of tests. This might mean traces of cognition variance for the recognition tests and of divergent production for the recall tests. Katzenberger (1964) also used both kinds of tests systematically, with only one case of tests for one memory factor being confined to the recall type and none confined to the recognition type. Thus, tests of both recall and recognition types support the same memory factors.

Representative SI Memory Tests
In what follows, one or two tests are presented to represent each memory function. They were selected from among those most strongly loaded for their dominant factors and those whose properties are more clearly in accordance with SI trigram designations. Sample items are given for symbolic and semantic tests; items for visual tests are described, sample items being available in Guilford and Hoepfner (1971). The survey will follow the order in Table 8.1, row after row, from left to right within rows. As stated earlier, each test has two stages, a test page following a study page. It was also in two separately timed parts.

Memory for Units. For tests of MVU, the units have been in the form of geometric and quasi-geometric figures, human faces, and letter styles, in different tests. In Figure Recognition the fifteen figures on the study page are to be identified later scattered among thirty such figures on a test page. In Remembering Faces ten distinctive human heads are studied, to be recognized later among twenty. In Figure Letter Recognition fifteen letters, each in a distinctive typeface style,

---

[4]It has become known that Kamstra (1971) has found evidence that abilities emerging from analysis with a six-week retention interval were dependent upon abilities found with a three-week interval.

are studied. On the test page each item presents four styles for a given letter, one of which appeared on the study page.

Ability MAU has been reported by Feldman (1969), who used tests of the memory-span type, except that the examinees were told to repeat the elements of the series in any order. The latter specification probably avoided variance in memory for auditory systems. Incidentally, Feldman was interested in abilities that might be related to beginning to learn to read, his Ss being first-grade children. He also found an MVU factor for his children.

A recognition test for MSU is Memory for Digital Units. A list of fifteen two-digit numbers is read aloud by the examiner five times, with the order of the numbers changed each time. The fifteen numbers are to be recognized among thirty on the test page. Memory for Listed Nonsense Words is another recognition test for MSU. Ss study a list of fifteen nonsense syllables, then attempt to recognize them among thirty. A parallel recall test is the same except S is to write the syllables he can remember in any order. In memory-for-units tests with visually presented material, sometimes the items are in a list and sometimes scattered about on the study page. This variation seems to make no difference in the factorial content of the test, so long as S is instructed in advance that he may present the items in his own order.

For ability MMU, Picture Memory presents sketches of twenty familiar objects scattered about the study page. Since S was instructed in advance that he would be expected to name the objects in a recall test, it was expected that the test would emphasize semantic-units memory rather than visual-units memory. The test did come out for MMU in the analysis. In a later study, to check on this, the test was analyzed along with others for MVU. It again came out for MMU and not for MVU. This is taken to mean that the memory in this test is for the objects, as such, and not for their appearances.

Memory for Classes. In tests for memory for classes, it is particularly necessary to control for memory for units. The principle of control has been to require S to recognize or to recall the class by using other members of the class. In other words, transposable class ideas were used.

In a test for MVC, S has to cognize the common elements in sets of three objects each and to show that he remembers the class idea by reproducing these elements in outline squares on the test page. One common element might be a principal diagonal; another might be an inscribed triangle.

In Memory for Nonsense Word Classes, S is given sets of three syllables each for study. As in all memory-for-classes tests, the cognition problems were made easy in order to rule out cognition variance, as in the sets NEC, NEP, NEF, and GUZ, GAZ, GYZ. S is then to recognize a new class member for each set in multiple-choice items such as: (1) GIS (2) GOX (3) NER (4) NUP. In Memory for Number Classes—Recall, S is to state on the test page the nature of the classes he has encountered on the study page, which displays number sets such as "5 10 25" and 307 602 704. Any class description that shows that S has remembered a class idea is accepted.

Picture Class Memory was designed for MMC. Sets of three sketched objects each are presented, one example being composed of a sweater, a scarf, and a knitted cap. In a recognition test one of the three objects (for example, the cap) is paired with a new piece of clothing designed to keep the wearer warm (a knitted mitten). A parallel, mislead item presents another object from the same original set (the scarf) paired with an object of clothing not for the purpose of keeping the wearer warm (namely, a necktie).

Another MMC test is Classified Information. Sample sets for study are: SILK WOOL NYLON, and FISH HORSE SPIDER. The items for recognition in the retention test are RAYON COTTON FELT, and SNOW SLEET ICE. Although this test was loaded significantly on MMC, as expected, in other analyses it has also had significant loadings on CMC and MMI, each in a different analysis. The loading on CMC tells us that the cognition problems in the study page were not minimal for all Ss. The loading on MMI suggests the hypothesis that, in studying the sets of words, many Ss knew that they would be tested with other class members, and so adopted the strategy of thinking of other class members as they studied the sets. In the recognition tests, then, the implications that they had established functioned because some of the implied class members appeared in the test items. These results and the reasoning to which they lead suggest how an investigator can arrive at hypotheses concerning the ways in which Ss are attacking their tasks.

Memory for Relations. Like classes, relations are transposable, and advantage has been taken of this fact in order to control the functions of memory for units. For example, when a relation between two squares might be given for study, the same relation is to be recognized between two circles.

Common analogies tests have served well in all operational categories and with all contents. In Memory for Figural Analogies, S is to recognize in a new pair of figures a relation previously observed in another pair. A secondary loading for this test on MVT illustrates how some intended relations were evidently processed by some Ss as changes rather than relations. In future tests of MFR, care should be taken to use relations that cannot readily be seen as transformations.

A successful test for MSR was Memory for Name Relations, in

which ten relations, each replicated in three names of persons, were presented for study. Examples are: Robert Redding, Rose Reardon, and Roger Renshaw. A multiple-choice item for this relation reads: Roy (1) Rollins, (2) Revere, (3) Radford, (4) Young. The right answer, of course, is (2) Revere.

In Remembered Relations, a test for MMR, S is asked to complete sentences in accordance with other sentences that he has observed. On the study page he reads sentences such as "Diamonds are harder than coal." On the test page a multiple-choice item reads, "Coal is _____ than diamonds," and the blank is to be filled with one of these alternatives: (1) softer, (2) blacker, (3) less valuable, (4) none of these. The direction of the relation is changed in order to avoid success by remembering a particular word.

On the study page of another MMR test, Recalled Analogies, S sees incomplete analogies, such as NATIVE : TOURIST : : RESIDENT :_____, but he does not write the completion. On the test page the item "RESIDENT :_____," appears, and S is to write the completion. Although S reproduces a single word, remembering the relation should be necessary to ensure the right answer. From the results of the analysis it was possible to see whether MMU was indeed appreciably involved. The loading for this test on MMU was a reassuring .18.

Memory for Systems. The favorite kind of test for cognition of visual systems involves arrangements of objects in space. System-Shape Recognition presents for study a large rectangular frame with nine outlined, curvaceous blobs of different sizes and shapes arranged within it. Each retention-test item presents a much smaller rectangle with three smaller blobs within it, of the same shapes and same relative positions as three of those studied. These items are mixed with about the same number of other presentations that do not appear in the studied material.

In Monograms Recall, S studies five monograms, each containing the same three capital letters, for example, U, X, and P. On the test page he is to reproduce those different arrangements, being told only what three letters are to be used.

For the corresponding MAS function, Karlin (1941) proposed an ability that is a good candidate. It was related to Seashore's tests of Tonal Memory and Rhythms, as well as a test for muscial forms. Tonal Memory repeats short melodies (auditory systems) with one tone changed in each case, with S to say which one. Rhythm asks S to say whether two examples given in immediate succession are the same or different. The third test was not described.[5]

---

[5]Because of the requirement of judgments regarding identity of two systems, it is possible that the evaluative function EAS was involved, rather than, or in additon to, MAS.

In memory tests for either symbolic or semantic systems, serial order of items of information has been the favored kind of system, largely because of convenience. Where there is interest in memory for order and not for elements, a rearrangement task would be natural. Given the memorized items in scrambled order, S would try to order them correctly. But this historical method entails some scoring problems. In order to avoid this, other test formats have been employed.

For example, for ability MSS, in Memory for Nonsense Word Order, a list of syllables is given for study, followed by a kind of incomplete pair-comparison test. If the short sample list is GUJ KER NIK BAS, the test-item statements, to be answered by "Yes" or "No," are of the following type: 1. Did KER come before BAS? 2. Did NIK come before GUJ?

In Memory for Task Order the tasks to be remembered in order are tests that had just been taken in a single test booklet. The retention test presents fifteen pairs of test titles. In the same format, a Memory for Events test presents a list of common activities in order (activities such as talking on the telephone, feeding the dog, washing the car, and so on) followed by a list of "before-or-after" pairs for yes-no answers. Both were, of course, designed for MMS.

It is a significant fact that in all these systems-memory tests, and in other list-learning tests, there was no indication that simple associations between adjacent items of information were of any importance. Had such associations been functional, such list-learning tests should have shown significant loadings on the memory-for-implications factors (MVI, MSI, and MMI). They did not do so. It is possible, however, that the nature of the retention tests involving systems, as in the pair presentation, precluded showing such involvement. A test that gives each of the units except the last in scrambled order, to which S is to respond with the next in the memorized list if he can, would be more sensitive to a memory-for-implications factor. At any rate, the results thus far indicate that something other than simple item-to-item associations is being learned in serial-memorizing tasks.

Memory for Transformations. People remember changes, as such, as well as they remember the things that have changed, hence the memory-for-transformations abilities or functions. With visual information, movements are common changes that can be represented successfully in printed form as static, successive states. Such material is successful apparently because from the given information S can readily cognize the changes that have occurred.

In the best test found for MVT, Front-View Recognition, S studies sketches of ten solid figures, the front of each of which is turned at an angle. The front side of the object is labeled as such. S is to imagine how the object would look if it were turned and viewed directly from in front. The actual ten front views are shown on the test page, with a like number of other front views scrambled with them.

On the study page of Remembering Spatial Changes, a familiar object, such as a camera, is shown in two views A and B, which imply that a certain movement has taken place. In the corresponding test item, the A view is shown without the B view. Then a new object, such as a dinner pail or a doghouse, is given with a view similar to that of the A camera. The proper B view of the new object is to be found among the alternatives in the test item.

Transformations in symbolic information could be changes in spelling, or in other uses of letters, or in algebraic expressions that involve both letters and numbers. In order to avoid confounding with algebraic sophistication, non-mathematical letter and number tests have been preferred. A test called Memory for Misspellings was designed for MST, in which the study page presents fifteen familiar words all misspelled (for example, "ketl" and "boan," for "kettle" and "bone"). On the test page, each word is given correctly spelled, and S is to answer with the misspelled form that he has seen.

Memory for Hidden Transformations deals with words concealed within sentences. Given the following two sentences for study, S observes some transformations that are called to his attention: "The fa(t op)era singer danced." "You should loo(k ind)oors." On the test page, S is to say whether the transformations given in new sentences are the same as he saw before: "It puts him bac(k in d)ebt." "The ca(t op)ened the door." This is by no means a test of memory for words. S must remember, instead, how each word is formed when it is presented in a new sentence.

Believing that a pun is a semantic transformation, since there is a shift in meaning, the ARP developed a test called Remembering Puns. Given for study are sentences containing underlined pun words, underlined to call attention to the locations of the puns. A sample sentence is "The bird-loving bartender was arrested for contributing to the delinquency of a mynah." The corresponding test item gives: MYNAH _____ , in response to which S is to write the word with the other meaning, in this case, "minor," of course.

In Double Meanings, the same underlined word is used in two different senses in two sentences. For example: "She brought the groceries home in a paper bag." and "The hunter planned to go out and bag a deer." Among given pairs of words in the retention test appears the relevant pair, "sack—obtain," representing the two meanings by using direct synonyms. Other, irrelevant, pairs of words are also given. They could also represent symbols in common to pairs of meanings, such as "to wander—a city.")

Memory for Implications. The natural kind of test for memory for implications is of the paired-associates type. When such tests have been factor-analyzed in the more remote past, they have determined what was called a "rote-memory" or an "associative-memory" factor (French, 1951). But in more recent considerations it has been realized that two things were amiss. On the one hand, there could have been more than one such factor in different kinds of content, since three kinds of content had been used. On the other hand, as some bivariate investigators have observed, the completion form of the paired-associates task may involve memory for units as well as for implications. The ideal memory-for-implications task would seem to be in a matching format, asking S to connect *given* B terms of the pairs to given A terms. This is the format that my associates and I used. The completion form was also used, however, but only to determine the extent to which it covered memory-for-units variance.

For MVI, Paired Figure Recall *was* of the completion form, requiring S to draw a figure B to match a figure A, the two having been paired on a study page. There was no loading (actually it was −.05) for this test on factor MVU. This unexpected result may have been due to the fact that the B figures were absurdly simple, made that way so as not to tax S's drafting skills.

Two matching tests for MVI were Remembering Figure-Letter Pairs and Face-Shield Matching. The former paired simple flag figures with different typeface styles of one particular letter. The other paired faces with different family coats-of-arms.

Most of the historical "rote-memory" factors have probably been somewhere near ability MSI because syllables and names have been favorite kinds of material. The Number-Letter Association test pairs two-digit numbers for A terms with capital letters for B terms. In its first analysis (Tenopyr, Guilford, & Hoepfner, 1966) this test had a marginal loading of .28 on MSU. In a second analysis (Bradley, Hoepfner, & Guilford, 1969) it had a significant loading of .35 on MSU and another significant loading of .36 on MVI. These results suggest that, in spite of the use of familiar single-letter units as B terms, memory of which ones had appeared was of some importance and memory of the letters as figures also played a role in this test. The first of these two secondary loadings could probably be avoided by using a matching format, and the second one could be avoided by using two-letter or three-letter combinations as symbolic units.

MMI was found to be well represented by two completion tests and one of a matching type in an analysis of semantic-memory abilities (Brown, Guilford, & Hoepfner, 1968). Books and Authors pairs authors' names with titles of books they were presumed to have written. Each title implies an occupation, which S is to remember and to report in a recall test in response to the author's name. Although the A terms in this test are in symbolic content, the thing implied is a semantic unit. Where A and B terms are of different kinds of content, the content category of the thing implied seems to determine the content aspect of the function involved.

Paired-Associates Recall is of the traditional laboratory type. The pairs are of meaningful words, such as SUCCEED—HEAVY, with the later test item, SUCCEED— _____. There was a near-significant loading of .28 on the factor for MMU, where some relationship had been expected. Experience seems to show that where the B terms are rather familiar to *S*, one need not be greatly concerned about diversion of the paired-associates completion tests in the direction of memory for units. The matching format, however, should be generally preferred.

Discussion

The foregoing information has many useful implications. It should lead to clarification and replacement of some time-honored but less well-defined distinctions among kinds of memory. It should also point to neglected areas of investigation and should suggest some new techniques. I hope, too, that the nature of memory itself has been very much illuminated. In a more general way, the advantages of thinking in terms of an operational-informational point of view should have been demonstrated. The value of applying multivariate procedures of factor analysis in investigations of memory and learning becomes more apparent.

SI Views of Some Traditional Concepts. The translation of traditional terms concerning types of memory into SI terminology cannot be completely satisfying because the traditional terms have meant different things to different investigators. Roughly, "rote" memory has meant memory for symbolic information — nonsense syllables and the like. Meaningful memory has usually meant something close to memory for semantic information. Those who have investigated meaningful memory have sometimes accepted as an index of meaningfulness the number of associative responses commonly elicited by word stimuli. Semantic content is meaning. For an implicational (associative) description of meaning, see Guilford (1967).

Logical memory has been poorly defined. In contrast to the situation with regard to meaningful memory, there has been no operational index to use in determining whether the memorizing is logical. Inspection of studies coming under the heading of "logical memory" is likely to show that either relations or deductions are involved. Relations are, of course, one kind of SI product, and deductions are convergently produced implications, another kind of product.

But other SI categories may well be involved in what is called logical learning. I have suggested (Guilford, 1967) that logical phenomena include not only relations and implications, but also classes (in fact, all the other kind of products) in what may be called a "psycho-logic." Formal logic has already recognized some of the products. Psychologically we may as well go all the way. In addition to the greater comprehensiveness of this psycho-logic, it differs from formal logic in another important respect: while logicians have provided rules for reaching correct conclusions, psychologists should rather be concerned with determining the principles of logical operations. In accordance with this line of thinking, we arrive at the definition of intelligence as a systematic collection of functions for processing different kinds of information in various ways according to logical principles. As for the concept of "logical memory," the implication is that we forget that term, recognizing that all memory is logical in a new broader sense. Thus, the term should be replaced with finer distinctions along the lines of the products of information.

Psychologists have lived with the distinction between "verbal" and "nonverbal" memory without questioning what the genuine distinctions are. It is probable that "verbal memory" has usually meant semantic-memory functions. If verbal memory is restricted to semantic information, then the other, nonverbal, category is highly ambiguous—a catchall category. It is recommended that the nonsemantic categories of content replace the single "nonverbal" one.

Memory Problems and Learning Tasks. Those who specialize in human learning and memory should be able to recognize many places where SI functions and concepts apply. It is impossible to make an adequate survey of those applications in a paper of this scope. In addition to the basis for such a survey in the information provided here, a broader coverage is given in Guilford and Hoepfner (1971). Only a rough consideration of the literature on memory investigations, however, will show that bivariate studies have neglected some areas. With regard to content areas, memory for visual and auditory information has received relatively less attention, and to my knowledge nothing has been done knowingly on behavioral memory. The few studies on the relations of feelings to memory are really not investigations of memory for behavioral information.

As to kinds of products, much attention has been given to memory for implications, systems, and units. Some efforts have been devoted to memory for classes in connection with concept formation. Some factor-analytic findings have demonstrated the relevance of memory for classes in that context.[5] Very little attention has been given ex-

---

[5]See Chapter 6.

plicitly to the learning of relations and even less to memory for transformations. The latter oversight is serious in view of the demonstrations of relevance for transformation abilities in connection with learning to read (Kluever, 1968) and with learning from reading (Hoepfner, Guilford, & Bradley, 1968).[6] Transformations also make important contributions to creative thinking, for they provide an important basis for intellectual flexibility. Some leading scientists were in fairly good agreement that transformation abilities are among the most important to them in their work, when they were questioned about a number of SI abilities (Allen, Guilford, & Merrifield, 1960.)

From the examples of new tests that are cited, it can be seen that many novel formats were needed in order to exert the necessary controls for stressing the right operation, content, and product, in each case. Some of these controls can be readily applied in laboratory research on memory if investigations are along the lines of SI varieties of memory. If there is a sufficient number of subjects and if test tasks are well chosen, then the multivariate procedure of factor analysis can be applied in order to check on whether the controls have been effective. This check would show in what content and product areas the memory tasks lie, and whether other SI operations have been controlled. The results are also suggestive of what strategies the subjects had generally followed. Hypotheses thus derived can be tested in later experiments, or steps can be taken to prevent the possible recurrence of unwanted strategies and tactics.

The breakdown of memory functioning along the lines of the SI model offers much new leverage in envisaging problems of learning and memory in relation to development and to aging, types of pathology, and brain functioning. Research already performed on development and aging, in which tests along SI-ability lines have been used, shows that SI abilities grow at different rates, come to maximal, mature status at different ages, begin to decline at different ages, and show different rates of decline, as seen in results summarized elsewhere (Guilford, 1967).[8] The same resource includes a summary of results showing possibilities of relating SI abilities to pathology, particularly agnosias and aphasias.

General Views of Memory. Informational views of memory, which seem to be growing in popularity, can be elaborated and systematized along the lines of SI concepts. Information seems to be stored in the same form in which it is cognized, and is retrieved in the same form as

---

[6]See also Chapter 7.
[8]See also Chapter 11.

to content and product. But there is also flexibility during retention and at the time of retrieval. Certain qualitative changes during retention have been pointed out, such as leveling and sharpening. A tendency for the dropping out of details and the better survival of general aspects has been noted for an even longer time. This may mean a priority for the products of classes and systems in memory, and indicates their usefulness as cues operating in the retrieval of units and other components.

Some important questions remain. Why are there so many relatively independent memory abilities or functions, as shown by factor analysis? Are there possibly more general, higher-order factorial memory abilities, each perhaps representing a whole content category or a whole product category? Is there even a completely general memory ability? If there are such more general memory abilities, they are evidently much weaker in terms of variances that they could show. Tests differing even in only one parameter of the SI model have low correlations, generally near zero.

The general picture that has been obtained suggests some potent interaction effects, which hinder transfers of functioning beyond SI cell limits. G. A. Ferguson (1956) proposed the hypothesis that, generally, abilities differentiated by factor analysis arise in a culture by reason of characteristic transfer effects. This means that transfer of developed skills, such as a factorial ability, is very much restricted within the bounds of that skill. This does not mean that the skill is completely specific; there is generality of some scope, but less than might be expected. It may be that certain educational procedures could help to extend that scope, particularly if the possibility is pointed out to the learner. This line of thinking opens up whole ranges of problems on transfer effects not envisaged by either S-R or associational theory.

The general informational view suggests many other consequences, one of which is concerned with interferences or inhibitions in learning. Information is a matter of discriminations, every item having its unique existence. The fixation of information in the operation of memory usually calls for redundancy in the form of repetition of input. It can be suggested that an important role of this redundancy is to sharpen discriminations, thus increasing the amount of information in that sense. Interferences in learning mean confusions of information, or incomplete discriminations. This hypothesis is supported by the common finding that overlearned information resists interferences, proactive and retroactive.

Another general implication of the SI view is a definition of learning. From this point of view, learning involves acquisition and fixation of information in storage. Acquisition means structuring or restructuring of items of information (cognition), with improved discriminations. The other operations, production and evaluation, may make some contributions to learning, as in problem solving. Tradition has often defined intelligence as *the* ability to learn. Another statement puts things more accurately: intelligence includes abilities for learning. The implication for education is that attention should be given to all SI abilities wherever they are relevant. Meeker (1969) has already taken large steps in this direction.

Summary

The distinct memory abilities or functions that have been demonstrated in recent years by factor analysis of individual differences in learning-and-memory tasks have much to offer to all who are concerned with investigation in this area. The Structure of Intellect, in which the memory functions have been organized, is proposed as a frame of reference. The model provides a much better defined set of concepts to apply in the domain of memory investigations. It can also generate new problems and illuminate results. New memory-test techniques suggest ways of exerting better experimental controls.

Particulars were illustrated by citing many examples of tests representing the various abilities. Neglected areas of research were pointed out. Suggestions were made concerning the nature of memory and learning, and concerning some applications to education and other fields.

Part III
The Higher
Mental Processes

Probably in no psychological area have there been so many persistent, ill-defined, highly ambiguous concepts as those known as the "higher mental processes." It is the major objective of the following chapters to propose some replacements, in the form of well-anchored, operational concepts—operational in the broad sense of the term. They are anchored in the categories of the Structure-of-Intellect model, which refer to the kinds of tasks that it takes to represent them.

In Chapter 6 the concept of "concept" itself was given a localized connection with the SI product of class. Other traditional concepts usually cannot be so clearly delimited, but sets of SI connections are more or less reasonably evident for all of them. That ancient and honorable term "reasoning" is rather amorphous, in contrast with the systematic collection of SI functions. The concepts of induction and deduction, however, can be aligned with two of the SI operation categories. But "problem solving" really "covers the waterfront." When viewed analytically in terms of SI categories and their combinations, certain aspects of problem solving can be localized. Decision making can also be accounted for by virtue of its common identification with problem solving. Some of the more special concepts arising from modern experimental research, such as "search model" and "functional fixedness," have logical connections with the SI model.

It will be demonstrated in general terms how the mental activity in any task that is proposed as an example of one of such traditional events as reasoning or problem solving, can be subjected to experimental factor analysis, along with marker tests for the hypothesized factors, thus determining the SI components of the proposed task. Again, the investigation of how individuals differ systematically in their functioning can inform us regarding what functions they have in common. Special attention is given to creative thinking as well as to problem solving. In general, processes of creative thinking have been traced primarily to the SI operation of divergent production—across all kinds of informational contents and all informational products—and also to the SI product of transformation—across all operation and all content categories.

Much creative thinking occurs in a setting of problem solving, which usually encompasses a broader set of mental events involving any of the SI operations, contents, and products, depending upon the nature of the problem. A model for problem-solving episodes has been developed—the Structure-of-Intellect Problem-Solving (SIPS) model—to account for the flow of events in a complete problem-solving episode.

Recognizing that most cases of decision making involve problem-solving steps, the SIPS model is also applied to this common event, with emphasis on the operation of evaluation. The role of SI functions in connection with decision making happens to be brought out in connection with the treatment of that subject in relation to aging.

Chapter 9

BASIC CONCEPTUAL PROBLEMS IN THE PSYCHOLOGY OF THINKING[1]

Of all the baffling problems that have fallen to the lot of the psychologist, those pertaining to human thinking have been the most frustrating. Nevertheless, no psychological problems are more important. For if we are to make the most of our intellectual resources to meet the challenging problems in this complex world, it is imperative that we know more about the processes of human thinking. This paper is in recognition of the need for effort to gain the required understanding.

The history of psychology exhibits a number of abortive attempts to reach a more significant and more useful comprehension of thinking. Wundt is said to have thrown up his hands, recognizing the inadequacy of his analytical, introspective method to cope with the problem (Boring, 1950). Titchener and Külpe refused to accept the limitations of that approach (Titchener, 1909). Titchener, however, contributed practically nothing when he attempted to account for thinking in terms of sensations and images. Külpe and his associates fared somewhat better when they sought descriptions in other kinds of terms. But in still taking the introspective route they were up against the fact that most thinking activity is well beyond direct observation. The glimpses that Külpe's imageless-thought group caught did yield a few reasonably descriptive concepts. We may say, however, that they barely scratched the surface of the problem.

Watson (1929) also failed when he attempted to catch the essence of

[1]Adapted from the *Annals of the New York Academy of Sciences*, 1960, 91, 6-21, with extensive revisions to bring the material up to date.

thinking in terms of speech reactions and other muscular movements. The difficulty with a purely peripheral approach to thinking is
that the phenomenon is essentially central. Although we can learn
much regarding thinking processes by the examination of stimulus
conditions, the motor reactions of a thinking individual seem to bear
very little relation to thinking, as such, at least in unique ways that
would enable us to infer much regarding thinking operations from
muscular contractions.

In spite of some promising beginnings in experimental approaches
to thinking, it seems that one of the critical needs has been for new
and more functional concepts. Concepts are tools used in research.
Full comprehension of the phenomena of a domain of investigation
does require answers to *how* and *why*. We cannot make substantial
progress toward answering these questions, however, without first
having answered the question of *what*.

What are the best conceptions of the phenomena in the domain of
thinking? What are the kinds of operations and processes and what
are the variables? Much experimentation has proceeded on the as-
sumption that we know what the fundamental operations are, too
often without questioning whether we could not have better conceptions. There is even inadequate definition of the operations that
are assumed to exist—that very frequently mentioned term "problem
solving," for example. What is the unique referent for "problem
solving"? No one can answer that question with any assurance of
wide agreement. Furthermore, psychologists have all too often fallen
victim to the semantic fallacy of assuming that one name means one
process. They have also not demanded empirical or operational concepts, which are essential for unambiguous communication.

Some of our working concepts have come to us as a part of our
philosophical heritage; such terms, for example, as "reasoning,"
"abstraction," "induction," "deduction," and "imagination." All of
these concepts suffer from the difficulties just mentioned. Of somewhat better status are concepts arising rather incidentally in connection with experimental investigations. Of Würzburg origin are the
concepts of "*Aufgabe*," "set," "determining tendency," and "schema,"
which, however, have not had significant survival, probably for good
reasons. From scattered sources we have had concepts such as "vi-
carious trial and error," "insight," "search model," and "functional
fixedness." These terms have also failed to gain general acceptance.
The paucity of adequate concepts of the better kinds has been a
serious handicap, and the few concepts that we have had cannot
support fully fruitful investigations of problems of thinking. In addition to their inadequacies, they do not fit into any unified theory of
thinking.

It is the major purpose of this paper to suggest a quite different approach, one that is uniquely suited to the generation of concepts, and one that answers questions of *what* kinds of thinking operations exist. The concepts arising from this approach are clearly empirically based and fit into a unified theory.

An Approach Through Individual Differences

The approach proposed is an application of the logic and the operations of factor analysis in an experimental manner. In the past, factor analysis has often been employed by those who are interested in problems of personality—that is to say, in problems of individual differences—and especially by those with some practical interests in vocational problems, for example. It has not been commonly recognized that factor analysis has potential value for contributing to knowledge of basic psychological facts and to general psychological theory. Only in recent years has the method demonstrated that it has much to offer in this direction.

Two General Approaches to Psychological Research. Experimental psychology through most of this century has operated on the basis of a model that has rarely been questioned. It is a stimulus-response model. Observed relationships have been restricted very much to connections between stimuli and responses. Laws are stated in the same terms. Following the pattern of analysis developed by the physical scientists, experimental psychologists have attempted to control all the independent variables except one, which is systematically varied.

The factor-analytic approach differs from the way of thinking and experimenting in two significant ways. On the one hand, instead of observing stimulus-response relationships, it examines the covariations among items of *response* information that are derived from individual differences in a population. This is done with a conviction that where individuals in a sample from a homogeneous population show relatively consistent variations in behavior in response to standardized situations, there is an underlying disposition or trait determining that phenomenon. The nature of that trait is inferred from the observable common features in the behavior.

The other major difference between the stimulus-response and the factorial approach is that, where the former favors the bivariate experiment, the latter capitalizes upon the multivariate design. In dealing with behavior, an advantage of the latter is its adaptability for coping with the great complexity of the phenomena to be described and understood. It takes individuals as they come (within specified groups) and, for the immediate purposes of the analysis, it need not be concerned with how they got that way. Bivariate experimental psychology should be concerned with this question, but except for carefully nurtured, inbred colonies of rats, for example, it can rarely control development, and does not do so. In the multivariate approach, within limits, such genetic variables can be ignored. This is not to say that genetic problems are unimportant. In fact, it can be said that genetic psychological problems, too, can be more meaningfully attacked if we know the *whats* of behavior, which factor analysis can supply.

A Factor-Analytic Experiment. A good factor-analytic experiment, whose objective is to learn something of psychological significance, conforms to several requirements. First, the investigator begins with hypotheses. In some area of behavior, such as that of visual perception, for example, he might hypothesize that visual depth perception is a unique function, distinct from all other visual-perceptual functions, as well as from all other functions. According to the hypothesis, individuals should be expected to differ from one another in performance in tests of visual depth perception without relation to performances in other kinds of tasks.

The investigator then develops three or more tests, each of which he thinks will indicate individual differences in the hypothesized ability, each test differing sufficiently from the others of this kind so that they are not just alternate forms of the same test. At this stage, the investigator probably has no basis for knowing whether there is, indeed, such a unique trait and to what extent it could determine individual differences in scores in the different tests. The investigator will hypothesize other visual-perception abilities, and perhaps abilities outside that area, and will likewise construct tests for those traits. He will expect the pattern of intercorrelations among all the tests so developed to tell him through the operations of factor analysis, which of his hypotheses are supported and which are not. Further description of a factor-analytic experiment can be found in Chapter 1.

Traditional Concepts and the SI Model

Many of the traditional concepts pertaining to thinking and related subjects find clear and localized places within the Structure-of-Intellect (SI) model.[2] Some of those concepts have, in effect, been carried over bodily; cognition and memory, for example, which refer to two operation categories in the SI model. The concept of judgment also appears, but under the synonym term of evaluation. Other traditional concepts have counterparts, but not so clearly on a one-to-one

---

[2]The frame of reference to be employed in what follows is the writer's SI model, which has been sketched in Chapter 2 and which has been treated at length elsewhere (Guilford 1967, 1977a; Guilford & Hoepfner, 1971).

basis. It should be added that cognition also plays some special roles in thinking and other complex processes.

Some Simpler Traditional Concepts. Some of the more limited, common concepts connected with thinking can be assigned to localized regions of the model of intellect, but some cannot. Let us consider first a few that can be localized, first of all the concept of "concept" itself. Concepts imply classes, and "class" is one of the products in the SI model, occupying an entire layer of functions. For the most part, tests for cognition of classes have called for recognition of familiar classes. It is probable that in such tests the examinee (*S*) is not required to construct classes, for that would call for productive activity. In tests of divergent production of classes, *S* is given a list of units and is asked to form as many different classes as he can, using each unit as many times as he wishes, in various classifications. Tests of the convergent production of classes are similar except that only one set of classes is possible, and *S* is so informed. Besides the functions pertaining to classes just mentioned, there are functions of memory and of evaluation, all of which involve concepts.[3]

Induction and deduction have been historical varieties of thinking. They have never been satisfactorily defined as psychological concepts. Induction has been characterized chiefly as a way of going beyond particular experiences to the knowing of something general or abstract. "Knowing something general or abstract" suggests the SI operation of cognition, hence we may locate induction in that category. If we ask which of the SI products represent something beyond the given, or something general, the first thought is of classes. If we think next of principles, such items of information could be in the form of relations or systems, two other SI products.[4] The idea of a particular pointing to something beyond itself suggests the product of implication. Thus, only the product of transformation has no clear claim as a case of induction. But we may as well drop "induction" as a scientific concept, since its phenomena are much better accounted for by cognition of most kinds of SI products.

Deduction is roughly defined as the drawing of logical conclusions from given information. There is usually the implication that the conclusions drawn are strongly, if not entirely, determined by the

---

[3]For evidence concerning the abilities or functions involving classes that play roles in the learning of concepts, see Chapter 6.

[4]In this connection it is interesting that the ability that Thurstone called "induction" has proved to be a confounding of SI abilities CSR (cognition of symbolic relations) and CSS (cognition of symbolic systems). Thurstone used only tests of symbolic content for his induction factor. Cognition applies to all kinds of content, however, and there is no reason for confining it thus.

given information. Drawing conclusions is an act of productive thinking. The fully determinined response means the SI convergent-production category.

Of the SI products to which the term deduction applies, only two, at first, seem to apply. One is in the convergent production of what Spearman called "correlates." His correlate is a unit of information that is needed to complete a relationship, where a relation and one other unit are given. The product involved is a relation. The production of a correlate is a conclusion in reasoning by analogy, and can therefore be regarded as a deduction.

The other kind of commonly observed deduction is a convergent production of an implication.[5] Given one or more items of information, another follows as day follows night. Although the convergent production of products other than implications and relations does not seem to fit the concept of deduction, the wider range of phenomena covered by convergent production, with six kinds of products applying, makes it seem a decidely better category of thinking. It covers what is commonly regarded as deduction and much more besides.

The concept of rigidity in thinking has been greatly illuminated by the discovery of factors of flexibility, rigidity's opposite pole (Frick, Guilford, Christensen, & Merrifield, 1959). Three kinds of flexibility have been revealed in connection with thinking. One of them was originally called "spontaneous flexibility" for the reason that it came out in connection with certain tests in which S can see no reason for being flexible. A typical score came from the Brick Uses test, in which S is told to list all the uses he can think of for a common brick. The flexibility score is the number of *kinds* of uses, not the total number of uses. It was eventually realized that kinds of uses are classes, and that the SI ability involved is DMC (divergent production of semantic classes). The flexibility involved is the freedom to go from one class to another; in not thinking in a rut, as shown in the extreme case where S stays in the same class.

Another kind of flexibility has been called "adaptive," for the reason that, in some tests at least, S is forced to change his direction of thinking in order to make a good score. It was eventually realized that the changes that occur are really transformations, which involve reinterpretations of information, and more than one revision may be necessary, as in a test that instructs S to revise items in several different ways. Conversely, the kind of rigidity involved is a tendency to be inhibited from making transformations. Both kinds of flexibil-

---

[5]A test composed of syllogisms to which S is to *supply* the conclusions is known to be primarily a measure of NMI (convergent production of semantic implications). There is no reason, however, to limit deduction to semantic content.

ity, spontaneous and adaptive, are in the divergent-production operation category, and all kinds of content apply. Thus, the two kinds of flexibility are divergent production of classes and transformations, respectively, for any kind of content.

It has been recognized that a third kind of factor accounts for a type of rigidity known as "functional fixedness." A classical experiment on this phenomenon has presented the problem of tying two ropes together when the two hang from the ceiling so far apart that *S* cannot grasp simultaneously both of them. Incidental objects lie on a table, among which one or two could serve as aids in the solution. Some *S*s pick up the pliers, tie them to the end of one rope, and swing the combination like a pendulum. With the free rope in one hand, the successful *S* catches the other on its approach swing.

One of the printed tests used for the same kind of ability is called *Gestalt Transformation,* which presents items like the following: "From which object could you most likely make a needle, (1) onion, (2) spice, (3) cabbage, (4) fish, (5) steak?" The keyed answer is "fish," with the thought that a bone from the fish, given an eye, would be most readily adaptable. This test has consistently helped to identify the factor first known as "redefinition." It is believed that those who do well in such a test can more readily define and redefine objects in order to adapt them to *specified* new uses. This ability is therefore NMT (convergent production of semantic transformations). Also found are other, parallel abilities, one pertaining to symbolic information (in a task calling for the rearrangement of letters in words according to rules) and one to visual content (in a task that presents complex figures, in which some lines must be reused to form simpler, hidden figures). All these abilities are in the transformation row of the convergent-production column of the SI model.

Reasoning and Problem Solving. A number of analyses of reasoning tests of various kinds have been made, leading to a number of factors that are not restrictively placeable in the SI model (Green, Guilford, Christensen, & Comrey, 1953; Kettner, Guilford, & Christensen, 1956 1959). The factors already discussed in connection with induction and deduction account for many of them, but it is very doubtful whether all the induction factors would be very obviously recognized as reasoning abilities. It is probably best to conclude that reasoning is so poorly defined psychologically that it cannot be given any unique location in the Structure of Intellect.

The same can be said for the even more ambiguous concept of problem solving. Because of the great interest in problem solving as a subject of psychological study, however, it is worth our while to consider what can be made of it in terms of the SI model. What is concluded regarding problem solving in this respect also applies in part to reasoning.

It should not require the results of factor analysis to lead to the conclusion that problems are extremely varied, and that solving them should depend upon different operations, contents, and products, depending upon the circumstances. There is no convincing evidence that there is a general problem-solving ability. From the factor-analytical point of view, the investigator's task is to identify the pattern of abilities that contribute to the solution of each type of problem. Such analyses have been done, but usually more incidentally than intentionally. Some examples of analyses of some typical problem-solving tests will be given.

One type of test is that of arithmetical reasoning. Repeatedly, the analysis of such a test reveals the differential involvement of two intellectual abilities plus relatively minor contributions of a few others. The leading component of the total variance can be attributed to the factor known for a long time as "general reasoning," which is now recognized as CMS (cognition of semantic systems). This factor commonly accounts for about 25 percent of the total variance (Guilford & Lacey, 1947; Kettner, Guilford, & Christensen, 1956). Its role seems to be to enable the problem solver to comprehend the problem as a system preparatory to solving it.

The second most prominent factor in arithmetical-reasoning tests Thurstone called "numerical facility."[6] The ability to do numerical operations rapidly and accurately has accounted for about 20 percent of the total variance. Other small contributors, usually to the extent of less than 10 percent each, are verbal comprehension—CMU (cognition of semantic units); spatial visualization—CVT (cognition of visual transformations); and spatial orientation—CVS (cognition of visual systems). An arithmetical problem is stated in verbal terms, hence the comprehension of word meanings makes some small differences in scores. Some problems either pertain to spatial arrangements involving distances and directions or the Ss think of the problems in visual terms, hence the variances in the two visual abilities. Spatial-orientation ability is a static appreciation of spatial arrangements whereas spatial visualization involves thinking dynamically about movements, rearrangements, and the like.

Some other factors are usually present in negligible amounts, and there is usually an appreciable amount of potentially predictable or true variance unaccounted for. One or two analyses suggest that, within the true variance sometimes accounted for, there may be appreciable components attributable to ability CMR (cognition of semantic relations), CSR (cognition of symbolic relations), EMR

---

[6]Later analyses show that the Thurstone factor of numerical facility is actually a confounding of two SI abilities — NSI (convergent production of symbolic implications) and the parallel MSI (memory for symbolic implications).

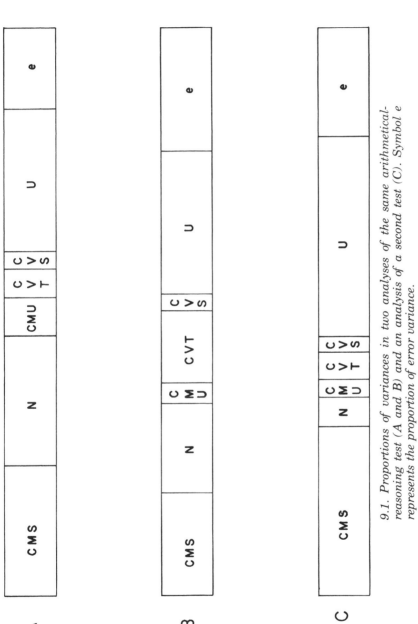

9.1. Proportions of variances in two analyses of the same arithmetical-reasoning test (A and B) and an analysis of a second test (C). Symbol e represents the proportion of error variance.

(evaluation of semantic relations), and EMI (evaluation of semantic implications). From the prominence of cognition abilities in these lists, one could readily infer that, in solving arithmetical problems, understanding the nature of the problem is a large part of the battle. Four of the SI operations are apparently involved, but the small degree of relevance for production abilities is somewhat surprising. Of the SI products, only that for classes is absent from the list of abilities mentioned—systems, transformations, and implications seeming most relevant. These findings illustrate just how intellectually complex one kind of problem solving can be. Other kinds of problems may well depend upon still other intellectual resources.

Figure 9.1 is designed to illustrate some of these, and other, points. Diagrams A and B represent results of analysis of the same form of arithmetical-reasoning test in two different samples, showing how much consistency may be expected in studies of the factorial composition of a test. Such consistency depends to a large extend upon using samples from the same population and using similar test batteries. The samples should also be large, perhaps as many as 200. Diagram C represents the results from an analysis of a different form of an arithmetical-reasoning test (Guilford & Zimmerman, 1956), which had been constructed with the aim of minimizing the variance in numerical facility, apparently with some success. The aim to emphasize CMS was largely realized. The variations in relative weights of the factors demonstrate how changes in tests of the same name and character may affect the demands that the tests make upon human resources. The larger proportion of unknown variances in the second test form (diagram C) reflects the fact that the analyzed battery was small, and only the five mentioned factors were at all accounted for.

In a particular study on problem solving, with different kinds of problems involved, there was interest in determining whether, after all, a very general problem-solving factor could be found (Merrifield, Guilford, Christensen, & Frick, 1960). Two tests called for the filling of gaps between initial and terminal information. In the Missing Links test an initial and a final word are given, with S to supply three words that make a reasonable chain of associations. For example, given the item: RED _____ _____ _____ BEER. S might insert the words: sunset, weather, cold.

A test entitled Transitions presents items in which the beginning and end of a short story are given, with S to fill the gap with reasonable events. In one method of scoring this test, the degree of coherence of S's contribution with the test's given information was emphasized. The main difference between these two tests appears to be in degree of complexity of information.

A Predicaments test presents in each item a not uncommon kind of difficulty. For example, a group going to a picnic takes the makings

MISSING LINKS: 45% OF VARIANCE ACCOUNTED FOR

PREDICAMENTS: 46% OF VARIANCE ACCOUNTED FOR

TRANSITIONS (COHERENCE): 48% OF VARIANCE ACCOUNTED FOR

9.2. *Examples of proportions of common-factor variances represented in three problem-solving tasks. The starred contributions can be regarded as significant. OC stands for other common-factor variances.*

for sandwiches, but finds that the cheese has not been sliced and nobody has a knife. there are available four objects: a harmonica, a thermos bottle, a book of matches, and a guitar. S is to tell two ways in which one or more of these objects could be used to slice the cheese.

The bar diagrams in Figure 9.2 show the proportions of the total variance for each kind of problem that can be attributed to each of several common factors, where there is enough to show separately.[7] The OC segment in each case stands for a combination of other factors, each contribution too weak to be shown separately. The starred factors were represented by their tests to degrees regarded as significant (with loadings of .30 or greater and thus with proportions of variance of .09 or more). It is likely that this level is above that required for *statistical* significance.

The proportions of the total-score variances accounted for in each test, as indicated by the communalities, were .45, .46, and .48, respectively. The proportions of total variances that could be accounted for, as estimated from the reliability coefficients, were .58, .55, and .46, respectively. From these figures we see that from 78 to 100 percent of the variances that could be accounted for were accounted for. These figures are mentioned not because they are necessarily regarded as precise, but because they illustrate several points and they show the kind of information that can be obtained by this approach.

The first thing to be noted about the results of this analysis is that there was no blanket problem-solving ability. On the contrary, these three tests, designed as problem-solving tasks, tended to be rather complex factorially, especially the one gap-filling task. Furthermore, the combinations of abilities involved in the different tests proved to be quite different. In this connection, the CMS factor that is so strong in arithmetical-reasoning tests, as shown in Figure 9.1, was conspicuously absent from these three tests. The explanation may be that in these three tests the structuring is very loose. What structure there is, is easy to comprehend.

Of the abilities that appear to be in common, CMI is most conspicuous, being significant in Predicaments. This ability is critical in the acts of seeing hypotheses, making predictions, and the like. Given information suggests other information. In Predicaments, it is possible that S must see connections between the given objects and slicing cheese. In the gap-filling tasks, one should expect that the given terminals would suggest the filler material. There was a bit of CMI showing in Transitions, but not much. The negligible weight of CMI in Missing Links is at first surprising, but it should be noted that S

---

[7]From data derived from an improved factor-rotation solution (Guilford & Hoepfner, 1971).

had to *produce* the fillers, and this fact shows up in a significant loading on factor NMI. Had *alternative* filler words been produced in each item, the ability should have been DMI.

Variances in creative-thinking abilities show up in connection with the two gap-filling tests, for DMU in Missing Links and NMT in Predicaments. This suggests that in those two tests some trial-and-error thinking was going on. One might expect some evaluation activity to go along with it, particularly in Missing Links, where there was less freedom. But apparently this aspect of the tasks was so easy that individual differences in evaluation abilities did not show up. It might be surprising that some divergent-thinking abilities did not show up in connection with the Predicaments task. There *was* some creative-thinking activity there, represented by NMT (convergent production of semantic transformations). It has been found that a task requiring the adaptation of a familiar object to an unusual use in order to solve a problem does involve NMT. Objects must be redefined in terms of their use to meet particular needs.

The large involvement of our old friend verbal comprehension (CMU) in Transitions reflects much need to deal with word meanings in writing connected discourse. One might have expected some need for CMU in Missing Links, but apparently the use of familiar words put a minimal demand on this ability. One should not particularly expect any CMU involvement in Predicaments.

A point regarding methodology should be mentioned here. Some investigators have maintained that the best way to derive an understanding of problem solving is to give subjects very complicated problems to solve; tasks that may require as long as three hours to complete. For most purposes this step seems to be definitely faulty technique, and quite unnecessary. The more complicated the problem, and the longer S has to work on it, the more the experimenter loses control and the less he can know about the meaning of the results. Scores from such tests have very low reliability, typically in the neighborhood of .25 (Chorness, 1959), hence there is little accuracy of measurement and little predictable variance.

Another practice that is experimentally bad, from the standpoint of ambiguity, is to use a test of problems, each of which differs in kind. The factor composition thus may change from item to item, and the total score is a very complex hodgepodge. We know much better what we are doing, and we also control better what the Ss are doing, if each item is relatively simple in its own way and the test is homogeneous. If we want to know the factorial composition of a complex problem-solving task, we should correlate scores from it with scores from factorially univocal (one-factor) tests.

Creative Thinking and Planning. Until comparatively recently, creative thinking had been a rarely used concept in psychology, and planning had no particular status except in popular usage. Planning partakes of some of the same properties as problem solving, for a plan is often the solution to a problem. Planning also suggests creative thinking because of its inventive aspects. We may well consider these two concepts together.

The general area of creative thinking has been well explored by factor analysis, with some results that are very enlightening, at least concerning the intellectual aspects involved. One of the initial expectations in the consideration of the subject pertained to fluency of thinking, the speed or facility with which an individual can produce ideas (Guilford, 1950). Another expectation stressed flexibility in thinking, or freedom from rigidity. Still another emphasized originality, an ability to produce novel ideas. The results have supported these expectations rather well (Wilson, Guilford, Christensen, & Lewis, 1954; Kettner, Guilford, & Christensen, 1959; Hoepfner & Guilford, 1966, for example).

The fluency factors that were found pertain to the speed of producing items of information to meet a need or situation (Christensen & Guilford, 1956). The items may be in any of the content areas and in any of the product categories of the SI model. The emphasis is on the plural, for multiple responses and variety of responses are special features of tests of fluency.

Reference was made earlier to two kinds of flexibility factors: spontaneous and adaptive. The former pertains to production of a variety of classes (SI ability DMC) and the latter to production of a variety of transformations (DMT), and other divergent-production-of-transformations abilities. Reference was also made to another type of flexibility, or freedom from functional fixedness, in the form of abilities for convergent production of transformations.

Some other expectations in the research were not fulfilled. The studies did not show an ability to analyze or an ability to synthesize to be unitary traits, although a number of tests of each kind were included in the analysis. Those tests went off in different directions, toward certain SI abilities. However, the failure to find analysis and synthesis as unitary abilities does not mean that such activities do not exist, any more than analysis shows that problem solving does not exist as an activity. Analysis and synthesis can be accounted for in terms of basic intellectual functions, like problem solving, depending upon the circumstances. What is commonly called analyzing a problem, for example, is likely to be cognition of relations or systems, among other things.

One kind of factor that should be classified with other creative-thinking abilities was found in a study of planning (Berger, Guilford, & Christensen, 1957). It was hypothesized that a planner, among other things, characteristically elaborates upon ideas, if he is to make the plan complete in every detail. A factor that could be described as an elaborative ability was found, and it has been interpreted as an ability to produce a variety of implications, specifically, divergent production of implications. One test called for the production of a somewhat elaborate plan to deal with a morale problem on a military base. Analysis showed that individual differences on this test depended upon abilities DMI, DMT, and DMU, plus others to smaller extents.

The various factors of fluency, flexibility, and elaboration constitute the category of divergent production, a kind of productive thinking that goes searching or that takes different directions, the end result being a variety of ideas, some of which are novel. It has, therefore, been common to identify the process of creative thinking with the category of divergent production.

This identification is easily defended, but it would overlook some other functions that are relevant to creative production. For example, the redefinition abilities, representing (in reverse) a form of rigidity, are placed in the convergent-production category. They are contributors to creative thinking because the transformation category is involved.

One of the initial hypotheses regarding creative thinking was that it presupposed a sensitivity to problems, on the grounds that if one does not appreciate that there is a problem he may not even start to think creatively. In tests designed for this eventuality, such a factor was indeed found. It was later given the SI placement of cognition of implications. Seeing a problem means seeing a need. And a need is something suggested by conditions as they are perceived.

If we consider the great variety of things that entail creative thinking in such fields as inventing, composing, writing, and theory construction, we have to recognize that many of the abilities in other SI categories also play roles. We can conclude that, although divergent production and transformations play crucial roles in creative production, in other respects the contributors to these kinds of activities are diverse, as in the case of problem solving.

Summary

Much of the difficulty encountered in the experimental investigation of thinking can be attributed to a critical deficiency of analytical functional concepts. We cannot very well discover how thinking operations proceed or why they do so until we know what the basic processes are.

Certain traditional concepts can be placed within the SI model, and they thus acquire empirical status. Induction is recognized as belonging within the operation category of cognition, and deduction within the category of convergent production. Three varieties of flexibility (versus rigidity) are recognized, two of them belonging in the divergent-production category and the third having to do with transformations in the convergent-production category. Other concepts that have not been so consistently connected with places within the model are reasoning, analysis, and synthesis. This is due to the multivariate nature of those concepts and their variable factorial compositions in different situations.

The same may be said of some concepts of even broader nature, such as problem solving, creative thinking, and planning. Being less standardized activities, they have even more widespread and relatively inconsistent affiliations with places in the model. The abilities most crucial for creative thinking appear in the divergent-production column and the transformations layer. Problem solving, being almost as broad as behavior itself, seems potentially related to a great many intellectual abilities, depending upon the circumstances. It is possible by factor analysis to determine the differential roles of the various intellectual functions in each kind of thinking activity as performed by each kind of population.

Chapter 10

More on Creative Thinking

and Problem Solving[1]

Creativity and Intelligence

Much has been said regarding the relation of creativity to intelligence. No answer to this question can be satisfactory unless we have clear defintions of both intelligence and creativity. These definitions will develop as we proceed with the discussion of this issue.

L. M. Terman, with the conception that his Stanford-Binet Scale measures an all-inclusive "general intelligence," thought that the secret of creativity, or creativness, in an individual is to be found in his IQ. Among many other things, a high IQ meant, for Terman, a high level of creative potential. But investigators who have studied the matter have invariably found only low correlations between IQ and performance in relatively new kinds of tests that are aimed at creative aptitude and that have been found strongly related to criteria of creative performance.

The reason for this finding is simple. Abilities in the Structure-of-Intellect (SI) model most related to creative performance are represented little or none in intelligence scales. Actually, only a very few of the SI abilities are touched by ordinary IQ scales. With respect to kinds of SI operations, IQ scales include mostly tests devoted to cognition, with some attention to memory, less to convergent production and evaluation, and practically none to divergent production. As for kinds of content, IQ tests emphasize semantic abilities, with some attention to symbolic and visual information but little or none

---

[1]Adapted from the author's article "The psychology of creative thinking," in *The Synoptic Thinker,* Aug.-Sept. 1977, 7-16.

to behavioral or auditory information. With regard to kinds of products, they overwhelmingly emphasize units and systems, give some incidental attention to implications, and very much ignore transformations and classes.

In creative thinking all the SI operations play roles, with divergent production being especially relevant. Any of the kinds of products may be involved, depending upon the nature of the task, with transformations being especially important, for they provide a basis for flexibility and originality.

The significance of the kinds of content lies first in the fact that problems and their solutions tend to lie within the different content categories. The problems of the inventor, the architect, the engineer, and the artist are largely in visual terms. Problems of the composer, the arranger, and the artistic musical performer are obviously fully or partially within the auditory area. Mathematical problems are largely in symbolic terms, but also involve visual thinking, as with geometry and functional relationship. Behavioral problems are more likely to be encountered by parents, teachers, police officers, court officials, and managers, all of whom must deal with people. Semantic problems are the most common, although they are of special concern for writers, scientists, planners, and, in fact, for all of us. Because abilities differ along the lines of the SI content categories, we should not expect to find that a creative person is highly creative in all fields. Individuals tend to specialize along content lines.

Although thinking tends to be channeled in terms of one language or code, there is no requirement that we stick to one category. We often do cross content boundaries, resorting to translations, as in solving a verbally comprehended problem mathematically. Thus, in whatever content area the problem lies, the solver has the option of translating it into the channel in which his abilities are stronger. It would thus pay for the person to know in which channels he is strongest.

The preceding discussion implies definitions of both intelligence and creativity. More definitely, intelligence is a systematic collection of abilities or mental functions for processing different kinds of information in various ways. In its present form the SI model involves thirty kinds of information. The ways of processing are the five kinds of operations. The term "creativity" has commonly been used in two ways: (1) to denote potentiality or predispositions of individuals for creative thinking, and (2) to refer to the process of creative thinking itself. Thinking is creative when output is novel—novel to the thinker, that is.

Some writers would add that the output must be relevant, a restriction intended to exclude the ravings of the insane, for example, for such output does have novelty. The label of "relevant" can be interpreted as "logical," with the thought that the normal brain generally operates according to logical principles—according to the psycho-logic that is based upon the SI products. In order to make this state-ment more plausible, it can be said that we do operate with classes and class members, with relations and relata, and implications are rather generally recognized logical connections. The brain is indeed a logical device, quasi-mathematical in nature. Perhaps the disordered brain of the insane person has programmed itself to operate accord-ing to its own logical rules.

Steps in Creative Thinking and Problem Solving
The connections between creative thinking and problem solving that were taken for granted in previous discussions find support in the writings of others who have given serious attention to these two phenomena. It is recognized that there is problem-solving activity whenever an individual encounters a situation for which he has no adequate response ready to function among his repertoire of re-actions. If he tries at all to cope with the situation, he must adapt or modify known responses or he must invent new ones. These steps satisfy the definition of creative thinking that was given earlier. Thus, we can say that all problem solving involves some elements of creative thinking. It is not so clear that all creative thinking occurs in a general setting of problem solving, as in composing music, in writing a poem, or in painting a picture, for example. We could, of course, say that an artist's production is designed to meet a personal need for self-expression and in this sense is the solution to an inter-nally generated problem. Then again, artists are sometimes commis-sioned to create decorative products to adorn a building or to be used as articles of clothing.

The close resemblance between episodes of problem solving and creative thinking is evident in different writers' descriptions of these two activities. For example, John Dewey (1933) proposed the follow-ing steps in problem solving:

(1) a difficulty is felt;
(2) the difficulty is located and defined;
(3) possible solutions are suggested;
(4) consequences of these solutions are considered; and
(5) a solution is accepted, others having been rejected.

For an example of the steps distinguished in creative thinking, Graham Wallas (1945) suggested the following:

(1) preparation (information is gathered);
(2) incubation (information is allowed to simmer or ripen);
(3) illumination (solutions emerge); and

(4) verification (solutions are tested and elaborated).

After studying the performances of inventors, Rossman (1931) suggested a list similar to Dewey's:

(1) a need or difficulty is felt;
(2) the need is analysed; the problem is formulated;
(3) all available information is surveyed;
(4) solutions are formulated;
(5) solutions are critically examined;
(6) the new idea is formulated; and
(7) the new idea is tested.

The SIPS Model

In this day of the modern computer it is natural to think of an operational model in the form of a flow chart to represent a sequence of events. The human brain may, indeed, be regarded roughly as "that computer between our ears." This is not to say that the brain solves problems in just the same way as a computer does. The same kinds of outcomes may be accomplished, but very likely in somewhat different ways. In order to provide a general picture of how the brain does it, the Structure-of-Intellect Problem-Solving (SIPS) model was designed (Guilford, 1966). A revised version of it is shown in Figure 10.1.

The main flow of events is shown by the upper sequence of rectangles—each rectangle for one SI operation. Beginning at the extreme left there is a station for Input I, which initiates the series of problem-solving events. Two possible input sources are shown. E is for the environment and S is for the soma, or the individual's own body. The latter might be a pain or a feeling or emotion that the person is called upon to do something about. The second station is labeled as "Cognition I," which is merely awareness that a problem exists. Things are not as they should be. Something needs to be done. In Cognition II the brain structures the problem; it produces an awareness of the nature of the problem and what will be needed in order to solve it. This conception of the problem may include what Duncker once called a "search model," which provides the cues for retrieving needed information from memory storage.

To continue with the main sequence of events, if the search model is sufficiently clear and complete, calling for one, and only one, suitable answer, there may be a shifting of the action immediately to the convergent-production stage in Figure 10.1. If, however, the specifications for the one right answer are not very obvious, or the search model is not very precise, or, in fact, if it calls for a variety of answers, divergent production takes place. If the activity in either of these productive steps achieves answers, we have one or more "Outputs,"

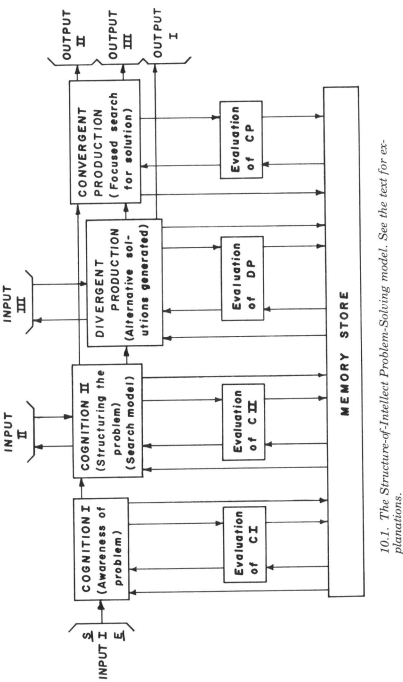

10.1. The Structure-of-Intellect Problem-Solving model. See the text for ex-
planations.

as indicated in the model. Output I occurs directly from divergent production only. Output II comes from convergent production only. Output III issues from convergent production following divergent production.

Before noting any further operations it should be observed that underlying everything is the memory store. Arrows pointing directly from it indicate points at which items of information in storage make contributions to ongoing events. Arrows pointing down to the memory store indicate the operation of memory—the act of putting items into storage. In this way a running account is kept of events that occur in the problem-solving episode. If it were not for this memory activity we could not remain oriented with respect to what is going on. We could not remember to avoid repeating errors or recall promising leads.

Evaluation occurs at all steps along the way, with checking on cognitions and productions. The checking may be solicited or it may be spontaneous, as arrows leading down to or up from the evaluation rectangles suggest. Memory storage may be involved either by way of supplying information needed in making evaluations or as a keeper of evaluation records. Some of the arrows between the main events and the memory store by-pass evaluation, except in the case of convergent production, where a retrieved item of information is unlikely to escape censorship. The by-passing is especially important in divergent production. Too much evaluation at this stage is likely to hamper retrieval of items of information, thus putting a damper on progress. Suspended judgement is very important during creative thinking, evaluation being postponed until a later occasion. With an evaluative, repressive attitude, needed items could be entirely missed.

One more kind of station in the SIPS model needs explanation. These stations are labeled Input II and Input III in Figure 10.1. They are to illustrate the points at which the problem solver feels the need of going back to the environment to obtain additional input. The arrow pointing upward in each case indicates the search for more environmental supply of information. The search is in part instigated by information already in the main stream of events. Some of the input may be unsolicited. Its incidental occurrence may spontaneously suggest solutions, as in the step of divergent production.

Another general feature of the SIPS model should be mentioned. In addition to the local series of looping events at the cognition and production steps, there may be much larger looping, such as occurs when all derived solutions are rejected and the solver goes all the way back to the Cognition II step. Back-tracking may, of course, occur at any point. All these looping events would call for some complicating of the model. The diagram in Figure 10.1 is an idealized picture, given as much simplicity as would be justifiable for a complete problem-solving episode.

Roles of SI Products in Problem Solving

Not represented in the SIPS model are certain dependencies of problem solving upon other concepts of the SI model. The products, especially, have some significant roles that should be mentioned. Starting with the first major event, Cognition I, or the awareness that a problem exists, the product is an implication. This fact was demonstrated clearly and repeatedly when tests requiring seeing problems were factor analyzed. In the Apparatus Test, for example, the examinee is asked to state what two things he sees wrong or in need of improving in a common object like the telephone or a typewriter. If he can name only a few faults, he is evidently low in the SI ability of CMI (cognition of semantic implications). Seeing faults with social customs or institutions indicates the same ability.

Another kind of event in problem solving in which implications play roles is in the formation of hypotheses. This occurs both in attempting to get a good grasp of the nature of the problem and in foreseeing consequences of suggested solutions. A hypothesis is a projected guess coming from what is already known. The person who is more ready to produce a number of different hypotheses is high in ability for divergent production of implications, in any content area. Foresight is a matter of cognition of implications.

Implications are sometimes very important toward the end of problem solving. Very often some elaborating activity is needed in order to make the solution entirely satisfactory. An artist adds finishing touches to his painting, each largely implied by what is already there. A plan of action is usually conceived first in a general outline form, and a number of more detailed steps are needed in order to make the plan work. These details are implied by the outline. Beyond this, there may be some supplementary steps needed in order to implement the plan. Elaboration is divergent production of implications.

In structuring a problem, in understanding it, the SI products most commonly involved are classes, relations, and systems. A doctor must decide what treatment to prescribe for a patient, for example. The diagnosis puts the patient in a certain medical class, thus providing a particular search model. Having reached a diagnosis, the doctor selects from his memory store a certain treatment or class of treatments, convergently produced. The class becomes a search model from which several alternative specific treatments may be divergently produced. It may require further tests to determine which particular treatment is best for the patient. For example, the patient may be diabetic, which would preclude certain treatments, thus narrowing the class.

Classes play roles also in the production phases of problem solving. An example of divergent production from a class was just given. A class thus serves as a cue for retrieval of information from storage. In this connection, it is well for the solver to employ a large, inclusive class to begin with. Sometimes the class idea is so small that it excludes the needed solution. If the problem should call for the designing of a transportation system for a city, for example, it might be a handicap to begin by asking "What kind of train should be used?" A better tactic would be to ask, "How could we move people efficiently, economically, and attractively?" Such an approach opens the gate to a much wider range of possibilities.

Another aspect of the use of classes as search models is the question of flexibility. Can the problem solver shift readily from one class model to another? This feature is illustrated by a simple psychological test used in connection with creative-thinking abilities. In this test the examinee is instructed to list all the uses he can think of for a common brick. At the one extreme, some examinees limit their responses to using bricks as building materials. Others are more or less inclined to shift their uses to some unusual purposes. The latter have more of the ability DMC (divergent production of semantic classes); they shift readily from class to class. This interpretation of the ability is justified by the fact that those who score high in this test are also likely to do well in a test that presents a list of perhaps a dozen objects and asks the examinee to classify them and then reclassify them in several different ways. It is sometimes said that a common disease of uncreative persons is a "hardening of the categories." They lack flexibility with respect to classes, at least in the semantic area.

Since classes are so often useful in retrieving information from storage, an important inference is that, in order to facilitate the operation of retrieval in either divergent or convergent production, items of information should be committed to memory storage well classified. In order to avoid rigid classifications, the same item should be identified with a number of different classes. The memory store thus becomes a file rather than a pile. Things are well labeled in different ways. As in a library, all items in the memory store should have their useful call numbers.

While some search models are in the form of classes, others are relations (the solution needed must satisfy a certain relation). A simple kind of arithmetical problem illustrates this kind of model. One such problem reads, "If a certain vertical post six meters tall casts a shadow two meters long, how tall is a tree that casts a shadow of five meters?" Such problems, of course, call for reasoning by analogy, a tactic that is sometimes recommended for creative thinkers wherever it can apply. Sometimes where a relation is not obvious one can be invented, and a useful search model is thus achieved.

Systems also function in constructing a search model and in producing a solution. If at all complex, the problem must be conceived as a system. For example, the arithmetical problem just cited involves only one relation but two pairs of numerical values. It could be complicated even further if we asked for the answers in units other than meters. The solution to such a problem involves a sequence of numerical steps and is thus a system.

Another example in which both the problem and the solution are systems would be in a business organization that has its table of organization and its standing operating procedures, and in which something has gone wrong—profits are dangerously low. This circumstance calls for a reexamination of both systems. It may be that one or both of the systems need to be revised, or that at least one new system is needed. In either case, the faulty organization or the faulty operating procedures must be understood as a system and a different one must be constructed.

Revising a system, or anything else, is an instance of the occurrence of a transformation. It has been emphasized that transformations provide an important key to flexibility and originality. It is sometimes said, unthinkingly, that "there is nothing new under the sun." Although it is true that any mental event is in part dependent upon old ones, an item of information that is changed brings something new into existence, at least for the thinker himself. The transformation itself is an item of information that is new to him. It should be added that changes can occur in one's understanding of the problem as well as in producing solutions for it.

Thus, all of the SI products play their various roles in problem solving, as well as all the SI operations. Problems can arise in any of the SI content areas and can be conceived in those areas. Problems and their solutions are often translated into other content categories, however, as when a semantically conceived problem is put in mathematical terms, which could be either symbolic or visual, or when a psychological problem of a patient—a behavioral conception—is translated into semantic terms with the aid of a psychologist or a psychiatrist, thus making things more manageable.

Chapter 11

Intellectual Aspects

of Decision Making[1]

Like problem solving, which it very closely resembles, decision making is often a quite complex affair psychologically. The term itself came from the popular vocabulary and should not be accepted as a technical psychological concept until it is given a good empirical foundation. I shall devote most of my efforts in this paper to giving the term some psychological content. The fact that I restrict myself to intellectual aspects does not mean that I do not recognize motivational features as well. This choice is from a long, intensive interest in intelligence.

Popular Varieties of Decision Making

Before going into more technical views of decision making, let us consider some varied kinds of situations in daily life in which decisions are ordinarily made. The range of situations and their possible consequences is enormous, all the way from answering the personal question, "Shall I eat an egg for breakfast?" to the question of historical importance, "Shall I (as chief executive of my country) order the dropping of an atomic bomb on the enemy?"

A young high-school graduate faces questions such as "Shall I spend four years in college or shall I look for a job?" If he goes to college, the major question is "Which curriculum shall I choose?" If he elects training in business administration, hopefully he eventually faces job offers. Which one shall he accept? Having selected one of them, which assignment in the organization should he request?

---

[1]Adapted with permission from a paper in A.T. Welford & J.E. Birren (eds.), *Decision making and age: interdisciplinary topics in gerontology.* Vol. 4 Basel: Karger, 1969.

In the political arena a young man decides which political party he should join. He decides to run for a particular office, chooses a campaign manager, and adopts a campaign strategy. After election, he decides which pieces of legislation he will work for, whose advice he should take, and how he will vote on each bill.

To extend examples of decision making, just to remind ourselves of its ubiquitousness and its generality, I will mention the more restricted area of psychophysical judgments. In the psychological laboratory many a mature person has been asked to judge whether this line is longer than that one, this weight is heavier that that one, or this light is redder than that one. Such decisions appear to be infinitely simpler than the kinds just mentioned, yet even these phenomena come under the general heading of "decision making," and they have presented the psychologist with problems that are far from simple when he attempts to understand them.

Decision Making as a Scientific Problem

Except for the case of psychophysical judgment just mentioned, and other transactions with the subject, serious interest in decision making developed outside the realm of psychology. It was persons concerned with economic problems who first saw the need for study of the subject, beginning with such social philosophers as Adam Smith and Jeremy Bentham and their concept of the "economic man."

Decision Making in Economics. The economic man was conceived to be all-knowing and all-wise. He made "rational" decisions, he had all the information that he needed, and he used that information so as to reach correct decisions. He was aware of all the options open to him and of the natural consequences of those alternatives. He was quite sensitive to the values of those outcomes, as if he had ordered them on a fine, numerical scale.

Decision Making in Administration. Very much later another group of theorists became interested in decision making. They were concerned with problems of administration of organizations, realizing that decisions are about the most important function of managers at all levels in the organization and that decisions may affect large numbers of individuals in many cases. They pointed out a distinction between the normative view of the economic pioneers, who were telling how decisions should ideally be made, and a new descriptive view, which attempts to find out how decisions are actually made. Among the leaders in this development have been Barnard (1938) and Simon (1947, 1957).

This group has considerably relaxed the assumptions originally made about the decision maker. The latter knows some of the obvious alternatives, but he often has to generate others. In this way he can know most of the important paths that are open to him, but he may still miss some. He can foresee or imagine some of the possible outcomes, but he can by no means regard all of them as being certain; they are only more or less likely to occur. This brings a stochastic aspect into the picture. There may be a real probability for the occurrence of any one outcome if all the pertinent facts are known, but the decision maker usually has to be content with his intuitive impression of the odds—his *subjective probability*. The decision maker senses probable values or utilities of the various possible outcomes. He may possibly rank or scale these utilities. Finally, the decision maker has criteria by which he is guided in accepting an outcome that would be satisfying to him under the circumstances. He will settle for what he can achieve, if necessary, or he will demand only outcomes of highest value.

Decision Making in Statistics. Another group of thinkers who came upon problems of human decisions has been the statisticians. Chief among them has been R. A. Fisher, who developed and promoted the procedures whereby decisions could be reached between alternative hypotheses, after adopting certain rules of the statistical game. With t and F tests, one can accept or reject what are usually known as "null" hypotheses, and, from the obtained statistical results, one is informed concerning the degree of probability of having made a wrong decision. More recently, Savage (1954) has made a case for application of the Baysian theorem, which involves an element of subjective probability in reaching decisions.

Game theory. Not to be overlooked in connection with more recent treatment of decision problems in economics is "game theory," originating with von Neuman and Morgenstern (1944). This approach considers the decision maker within the give and take of economic events, as betweeen bartering individuals who make moves and countermoves. Here one encounters successions of decisions, one dependent upon the other.

The Psychologist's Concern with Decision Making

Attention of psychologists to problems of decision making has appeared mainly within the past twenty years in the work of Cohen and Hansel (1956, 1958, 1964), of Edwards (1954, 1961), and of Luce and Raiffa (Luce, 1959; Luce & Raiffa, 1957). Scientific interest in any phenomenon adopts the goal of description, and in the case of psychology it is description of the decision maker's mental operations. It will have to suffice here to mention only some of the major problems as psychologists have seen them.

Variables in Decision Making. Two of the important situational variables recognized and utilized in psychological studies have been the degree of risk in connection with alternatives and the degree of uncertainty or lack of information. Efforts have been made to derive some principles, and a few have been stated, in connection with maximizing utility and with minimizing risk. The expressions "maximizing" and "minimizing" suggest mathematical possibilities, which have been pursued vigorously. This approach has made necessary the measurement of such variables as subjective probability and utility.

Motivational problems have pertained to the phenomenon of goal setting and goal changes within the decision-making situation. Goal setting is concerned with the question of *what* is to be achieved and also with aspiration level, which sets standards of anticipated satisfactions to be reached. Motivational conditions also involve the utilities of the various possible outcomes.

Intellectual problems have been less well recognized and less often given attention. Although to say that decisions have their rational aspects gives them intellectual implications, there has been little speculation as to what the intellectual involvements are or what they entail.

In part, this situation may be attributed to the lack of a theory or a systematic frame of reference for intelligence or intellect. In part it has been due to the psychologist's taking his cue from those who have emphasized decisions in risk and gambling contexts. It will be shown later that a much broader conception is needed if all psychological aspects are to receive attention.

Decisions are rational to the extent that they are based upon known information and the appropriate use of that information. We can take a large step toward accounting for the intellectual aspects by emphasizing the fact that the decision maker often generates alternatives—they are not always given by the situation. There is also the fact that, knowing the alternatives, the decision maker must generate logically possible outcomes. More than that, he must go through steps of evaluating the outcomes. In other words, he must cognize probabilities in the situation, and he must try to make his subjective probabilities approach the real probabilities.

Relations to Intelligence. Since conceptions of intelligence have come about mostly through investigations of individual differences, let us first consider some attempts to study decision making through this approach. There have been some references of possible roles of certain variables of individual differences, or traits, but not much actual investigation. One important study was made by Kogan and Wallach (1964). They studied ways in which variables in reactions to risk, as in betting, and strategies in dealing with odds and preferences for different odds, are related to other personal variables, including sex, defensiveness, and anxiety level. The same variables were also related to a measure of intelligence, a score on the Scholastic Aptitude Test. Very few relationships were found. For the entire group of student subjects the highest correlations were only about .20.

When the sample of subjects was fractioned into smaller groups, however, it was found that for low-anxiety and low-defensive men there were moderate degrees of correlation between the intelligence score and risk-taking scores. For this group it was concluded that the high-risking individual takes more chances in guessing answers to multiple-choice items (of which the Scholastic Aptitude Test was composed) and that, when they guess they have better-than-chance success. High-anxiety men are not so likely to guess, and when they do, they are more likely to be wrong. These considerations led the investigators to the curious conclusion that high status in intelligence tests is largely a matter of risk taking, at least when the items are of the multiple-choice form. They preferred this hypothesis to what would probably be the more popular one, that the more intelligent the individual the more self-confident he is about taking risks and the more justified he is in doing so.

Be this as it may, from this or from other investigations of decision making we have a very limited picture of the relations of intelligence to any of the aspects of risk-taking behavior. Previous efforts of this kind have been further limited by the restricted aspects of intelligence that is measured by means of traditional intelligence tests. We shall see later that, with a much broader inclusion of intellectual abilities (most of which are missed by conventional tests), there are many reasonable possibilities for substantial involvements of intellectual abilities in decision-making behavior. A much broader view of intelligence is demanded.

A Broad View of Intelligence: The SI Model. That broader view is furnished by the author's Structure-of-Intellect model.[2] In addition to offering a systematic presentation of known and conceivable intellectual abilities, the model presents taxonomic concepts for describing whole ranges of intellectual functioning. Many of those concepts are potentially useful in comprehending decision-making operations and in planning research on that subject.

Problem Solving: The SIPS Model. In a few places, writers on the subject of decision making have suggested that this phenomenon

---

[2]For a description of the model, see Chapter 2, particularly Figure 2.1.

belongs in the category of problem solving. The broad, catchall nature of the latter concept makes this allocation of decision making quite possible. With this identification the writer is in agreement, at least where the decision-making activity is relatively complex. Even when Hamlet made his famous statement, "To be or not to be," he was stating a problem. The reasonableness of the identification can be made more explicit by reference to the writer's Structure-of-Intellect Problem-Solving (SIPS) model.[3]

Decline of Decision-Making Abilities with Age. In the investigations of the relation of the goodness of decision making to chronological age, it would probably seem that the most direct approach would be to administer decision-making tasks to individuals of different age levels. Investigators who take an unanalytical view of personality would be particularly partial to this route. But there is no unique decision-making ability, any more than there is a single problem-solving ability. Any one decision-making test could therefore not represent all others. If one wanted the answer to the relations of all decision-making performance to age, there would be an almost infinite variety of tests that would have to be tried out.

If one takes the more analytical approach to decision-making potential, the approach based upon the SI abilities involved, the number of variables would be large, but it would be a finite number, and, with a logical selection, not so large after all. It is often questioned, of course, whether knowledge derived from investigations with component abilities can give us answers regarding complex activities. It could be argued that decision-making performance in any situation depends upon a chain of many links and that performance is no better than the weakest link. It is questionable whether this metaphor actually applies, however, for individuals have a penchant for compensating for their weaknesses. This principle is recognized when we apply a multiple-regression procedure in multiple-prediction problems. The fact that prediction from multiple sources does work in many situations seems to answer the question of whether analytical procedures are valid. In addition to the fact that the SI abilities offer a well-defined list of experimental variables with which to work, their relations to a comprehensive and logical framework should make them appealing.

Decision Making in Relation to Age

The system of SI abilities can serve well as a frame of reference in considering how abilities that should be involved in decision making are related to age. In the remainder of this paper, we shall consider

---

[3]For a description of this model, see Chapter 10, particularly Figure 10.1.

what appears to have been found with respect to relations of various SI abilities to age and the implications of these findings for decision making. Fortunately, investigators have very often used various kinds of single tests in their studies rather than composite tests with composite scores. On the basis of direct and indirect factor-analytic information it is possible to know or to hypothesize what SI abilities are dominant in the tests. We shall examine the findings in relation to operation and product categories of the SI model.[4]

Within the category of cognition abilities we find one very unusual exception to the general rule. This is the well-known ability of verbal comprehension, or cognition of semantic units, best measured by vocabulary tests. In comparison with most abilities, which show some declines in the ages past forty to fifty, verbal comprehension shows little normal decline. It may be recalled from an earlier statement that Kogan and Wallach (1964) found only a slight correlation between a measure of this ability (SAT verbal score) and certain scores for traits of risk taking. More pertinent would be correlations between scores for verbal comprehension and criteria of *effectiveness* of decision making.

Moderate declines in old age have been found in tests of two other semantic-cognition abilities: cognition of semantic classes and cognition of semantic systems. From these declines we should expect some weaknesses in seeing the classes to which semantically conceived problems belong and in structuring the problems. There are apparently more rapid declines in two corresponding symbolic systems— cognition of symbolic classes and cognition of symbolic systems— suggesting more convincingly similar weaknesses where problems are cast in mathematical terms. In the visual area of information there is evidence that abilities such as cognition of units, of systems (for the ability commonly known as spatial orientation), and of transformations (for the ability commonly known as spatial visualization) all start to decline at a relatively early age in adulthood, and that declines continue at an accelerated rate in old age. Decision making dependent upon visual thinking should thus become impaired.

All the declines in cognition abilities should help to account for the slower and the less certain learning, and the consequent lower retention by older individuals, since these declines entail reduced input efficiency. Considering all the results that we have on cognition abilities, it appears that there is least decline when the problem is in semantic terms, there is more decline when it is in symbolic terms,

---

[4]In the summarizing of results and conclusions here, there is much dependence upon a single source (Guilford, 1967), which in turn depended upon numerous, scattered sources.

and there is most decline in the case of visually conceived problems. No investigations are known, as yet, on declines with respect to cognition of implications or relations in connection with aging. Perhaps they, too, would show the same general trends as content varies.

The popular belief that elderly persons are especially weak in memory functioning is well known. Experiments show more marked interference effects in their short-term memory. It is possible, however, that much of what is known as short-term memory actually belongs in the category of cognition, in which case it is a weakness in input operations, not in retention operations, that is involved. Without cognition, no memory, obviously states a general principle.

Experimental results relating memory abilities to age have been limited to four SI abilities. Visual, symbolic, and semantic information have been involved, as have the three products of units, systems, and implications. Declines for units and systems have thus far seemed to be moderate, but they are noticeable after the ages of twenty-five to thirty. Wechsler's Digit Symbol test has been regarded as a memory test. Analysis shows that it represents, in part, memory for symbolic implications (each symbol being implied by its corresponding digit). The decline with age for this test is one of the most marked among the Wechsler tests. We cannot attribute all this unusual decline to the memory ability involved, for the test measures about equally strongly the SI ability of evaluation of symbolic units. The moderate involvement of this ability suggests that the subjects taking this test engage in considerable checking of their work as they go along. The decline, or a part of it, may be attributable to loss in this evaluation ability.

Declines have been found in tests of numerical operations, which have long been considered factorially as measures of an ability called "numerical facility." Recent analyses have shown, however, that numerical-operation tests share variance in two SI abilities: memory for symbolic implications and convergent production of symbolic implications. Conclusions as to relations to aging have to remain ambiguous in this case. There is still a great deal to be done in investigation of memory abilities in relation to aging, but we now have the measuring instruments that are needed for a systematic survey, with tests for twenty of the SI abilities in this category (the six memory-for-behavioral-information abilities not yet having been demonstrated factorially, and four of the auditory-memory abilities).

As indicated before, divergent-production (DP) abilities are concerned with the generation of alternatives. There are obvious roles for DP functions in decision making: in generating possible courses that might be taken and in generating the possible outcomes for each potential decision. Reports have indicated relations of age to at least five DP abilities, with three kinds of content and three kinds of products involved.

First to be mentioned are two tests of fluency, for DP of symbolic units (Thurstone's "word fluency") and DP of semantic units. Data for word-fluency tests show a typical age curve that peaks near the age of forty-five, with a rapid decline thereafter. In part the rapid decline may be due to the fact that fluency tests are speed tests. In word-fluency tests the subject must rapidly list words belonging to a specified class, such as words containing the letter N. For the corresponding semantic ability the curve peaks shortly after the age of thirty, with only a moderate decline thereafter. In tests for this ability the subject must rapidly list objects or ideas that belong to a specified class, such as things that are both soft and white. Here we have another case in which a semantic ability declines less rapidly than its parallel symbolic ability, the product being the same.

Another pair of abilities, one visual and the other semantic, are of interest, since they represent a form of fluency combined with a form of flexibility—two characteristics of creative thinking. Both abilities require a rapid shifting from class to class. A typical test in either case presents a set of units of information from which the subject is to form as many different classes as he can, using each unit more than once in reclassifying it. In a test for visual classes the units may be capital letters to be classified in terms of figural properties. A similar semantic test presents a set of familiar words that are to be grouped and regrouped as to meaning in alternative ways. The flexibility involved is a matter of shifting from class to class. The fluency is connected with the speed with which this can be done.

Nothing can be said about the age curve for the visual-flexibility function. It can only be concluded that older subjects often have difficulty in reclassifying concrete objects. The age curve for the corresponding semantic ability has been found by using other than the one described for the same ability. The curve shows a continued slow rise between the ages of twenty to forty, then an essentially level stretch to the age of fifty-five, then a moderate decline. It is characteristic of a number of DP abilities that have been studied in relation to age that the peak of the curve is past the age of thirty and that declines are relatively slow to come.

The use of one test involving flexibility with respect to transformations showed more decline than the test just mentioned. This visual test, Match Problems, presents in duplicate a set of squares whose sides are contructed of match sticks. The subject is to take away a specified number of matches, leaving a specified number of complete squares, and to solve the problem in different ways.

Information concerning declines in convergent-production functions is scanty and not very decisive. For our present purposes this deficit in knowledge is probably not serious. There would ordinarily be little apparent involvement in the more common instances of decision making, for convergent production requires full information, which rarely exists outside mathematics, logic, and scientific thinking. Some declines have been noted—some of them rapid—after the age of 50, as in the production of systems (indicated by the Wechsler Picture Arrangement test) and of transformations (indicated by a Hidden Figures test (with its Gottschaldt-figures type of problem). Less marked declines have been indicated for the production of relations, as in the Shipley Abstraction test and in verbal-analogies-completion tests.

The evaluation functions are of special interest because of the common feature of accepting or rejecting information in evaluation tests and in ordinary decision-making events. Unfortunately, the information on decline is very limited with respect to this SI operation category. For the two parallel abilities having to do with evaluation of visual units and symbolic units, there seems to be a slight decline to the age of forty-five, then a more rapid decline. Tests of the former ask the subject to say whether or not two pictured familiar objects are drawn exactly alike with respect to all details. Tests of the latter ask subjects to say whether two printed letter sets, two digit sets, or two names of persons are identical or different. Stating whether or not given units of information fulfill the required specifications for membership in a given class can also be used in testing for the evaluation-of-units abilities.

Some more complex decisions are involved in the Watson-Glaser Critical Thinking Ability test, which has been used at different age levels. The different parts of the test can be regarded as essentially ways of presenting syllogisms to be solved. In multiple-choice form this kind of test has been found to represent two SI abilities—evaluation of semantic relations and evaluations of semantic implication—about equally strongly. Conclusions derived from the use of this test would be ambiguous, at least so far as the relative involvements of relations and implications are concerned.

In the Watson-Glaser test the peak of performance appears between the ages of twenty and forty, after which there is a slow decline. Some characteristic qualitative observations have also been made. Elderly subjects tend to change premises to suit themselves and they sometimes elaborate on their opinions. They tend to give more extreme responses, such as "strongly agree" or "strongly disagree"; they sometimes show unjustified confidence in their own judgments; and they go astray relatively more often on items that involve personal implications.

The variations with respect to different SI products of information were touched upon in previous discussions, but there is one product that deserves special mention, information concerning its role in relation to age having come from various laboratory studies. This is the product of system. When elderly subjects are given laboratory tasks to perform, they show some weaknesses in abilities involving systems in various ways. In general, the more complex the task, the relatively greater is the difficulty of the task for the elderly. They show this in failure to understand procedures in a task and in relating different parts of the task to one another. They have difficulty in keeping a number of things in mind. Most of these difficulties seem to be in the area of *cognition* of systems, either visual or semantic, or both. Not being able to hold a number of things in mind might also show weakness in short-term memory, but earlier it was hypothesized that such a weakness might actually be in cognition, upon which memory depends.

Discussion

Previous paragraphs have pointed out many implications of intellectual abilities and their changes with age for decision making. A few general comments can be added.

Information and Age. There has been a longstanding popular belief that decisions would be most sound when coming from the aged, who are expected to be wise by virtue of accumulated years and accumulated experience. From an informational point of view in psychology there would seem to be support for this belief, in that good decisions depend upon having large funds of relevant information. There is also the fact that the individual's fund of information holds up well in old age, if it is in semantic form, and a large proportion of human decisions are made on the basis of semantic information. But it should be noted that the information must be relevant. It must be pertinent to the particular problem for which the decision is to be made. There has been some popular recognition of this point also— that individuals cannot be trusted to have dependable opinions outside their fields of knowledge. Furthermore, much pertinent information must be of a specialized nature in this world of frequently specialized problems.

Use of Information and Age. So much for the general role of stored information in decision making. We must also consider the things that must be done with that information. In general, stored information directly supports cognition, but it does not so readily support productive-thinking activities and evaluation, which are so important in problem solving and hence in decision making. Wisdom depends upon making good use of information as well as possessing it.

Thus, we need to consider, especially, the declines with age in the intellectual abilities of divergent and convergent production and evaluation. It was noted earlier that idea-generating functions, in the category of fluency or divergent production, remain at fairly high levels through the age of fifty, but all show some declines thereafter, sometimes with accelerating losses. It is not known how the individual's taking more time can compensate for losing facility in finding from his memory store the needed information for generating alternatives. The functions involving transformations show trends similar to those for fluency so far as our information goes. A lowering of these abilities should put a damper on making decisions that depart from tradition.

Insofar as we have information, the evaluation functions appear to start declining with age somewhat earlier than do the productive-thinking functions. It was mentioned earlier that the elderly tend to show too much confidence in their own opinions and too much personal bias. One would need to keep these considerations in mind in evaluating opinions of the elderly.

The elderly also exhibit a waning capacity for dealing with complexity, or a reduction in ability to deal with systems, especially at input stages. This means that either the elderly should not be given very complex problems, or presentations of problems should be simplified.

Summary

Decision making, a most common event in daily life, is so frequently encountered in problem solving that it can well be identified with that activity. The first serious attention to decision making from learned men in modern times was directed to its operations in economic and in managerial affairs, which helped to set a pattern for investigations of that phenomenon.

Psychologists' concern with the subject has been relatively recent. Their goal has been descriptive, with the hope of achieving generalized understanding of decision-making behavior. Some concentration has been on decisions made under risk and uncertainty, in which probabilities play prominent roles.

There has been little investigation of the role of intelligence in decision making, in spite of the fact that rational aspects have been prominently recognized from the beginning. Little relation has been found where intelligence has been operationally defined in terms of scores from traditional intelligence tests. The Structure-of-Intellect model, with its multitude of abilities, mostly untouched by orthodox intelligence tests, offers a promising theoretical basis for expecting many relationships. The link in theory is the SIPS (Structure-of-Intellect Problem-Solving) model.

Studies yielding information on decline in SI abilities offer some basis for inferences concerning weaknesses to be expected in decision making as a function of aging. Much more information of this kind is needed for a complete answer to the question of decision making in relation to age.

Part IV
Some Extensions

The remaining two chapters go beyond applications of SI concepts to the processes of intellectual functioning. It is pointed out that some of the proposed traits known as cognitive styles are in the nature of intellectual-control variables and that the directions of those controls are along the lines of SI categories. They could be regarded as executive intellectual functions. Some other cognitive styles represent different interests in, or preferences for, particular kinds of intellectual activities, also along SI lines.

Certain aspects of the SI model also apply to motivation, and to feelings and emotions. Self-generated behavioral information provides some of the basis for these connections. Dimensional models for feelings and for moods have been suggested, also having been derived through investigations of individual differences by multivariate methods. Relations of SI concepts to speech, education, and psychotherapy are also discussed. Needs for future research are pointed out.

Chapter 12

Intellectual Controls

Over the years, through studies of individual differences by correlational and factor-analytic procedures, quite a number of traits have been proposed under the general heading of "cognitive styles." One apparent instigating source has been the thinking of those who have been concerned with problems of "ego functioning" in psychoanalytical theory. The result has been a somewhat heterogeneous set of traits that appear to have effects on intellectual functioning in one way or another. A logical consideration of the proposed cognitive styles in connection with concepts of the Structure of Intellect appears to provide at least two common denominators for many of those trait variables.

There is general agreement that the cognitive styles are not intellectual abilities, although there is an occasional suggestion to the effect that some styles are to be so identified. The type of psychological test that reveals them is significantly different from tests of abilities, although some features are shared. Tests of abilities are aimed at determining *how well* certain kinds of tasks are performed—there is a value attached to the score. A style test, on the other hand, is concerned mainly with the *manner* in which the task is performed. It is sometimes pointed out that ability traits are unipolar, ranging from zero to a maximum evaluation, whereas a style trait is likely to be bipolar. Although one extreme of a dimension may be regarded as more valuable in some cases, generally, the two extremes simply indicate two opposite qualities.

Intellectual Executive Functions

Among the writers on the subject, almost all agree that cognitive styles have some determining effects on intellectual functioning.

Some go so far as to say that cognitive styles actually exert control over mental activity—see, for example, Broverman (1960), Santostefano (1969), and Wachtel (1972). Chapter 3 introduced the concept of executive functions, which were proposed as having control over patterned motor reactions. It is proposed here that there are also executive functions that have controls over intellectual events. It will be shown that some cognitive styles appear to fit this description, but some do not. Some examples of both kinds will be given, control variables first.

Field Independence versus Field Dependence. Among the cognitive styles, probably the best known is Witkin's Field Independence versus Field Dependence, which hereafter will be noted simply as FI. The tests that serve as empirical referents for this trait are well known, but not universally, so they will be briefly described here.

The Rod and Frame Test has *S* looking at a rectangular frame, within which is a rod. Before each trial, both rod and frame are tilted away from the vertical position with respect to *S*. *S*'s task is to manipulate a control until the rod is brought to the true vertical position with respect to his own body, which is sitting erect. The frame has somewhat diverting effects that are consistent for different observers. The Body Adjustment Test has *S* enclosed within a small room, which is tilted away from the vertical, and so is the chair in which *S* sits. *S* is to manipulate a control until he believes his chair is in the true vertical position.

The third test is very different in appearance, being in printed form. Each test item presents a somewhat complex line-drawing figure concealing a simpler figure that *S* is required to find and identify. The Gottschaldt figures provide the prototype for such hidden-figures tests.

The fact that there are consistent individual differences in the extent to which *S*s approach the true vertical positions in the first two tests and succeed in perceiving the hidden figures in the third test indicates that there is a trait of some kind. Intercorrelations among the three tests support this inference. Witkin's own interpretation of the trait is that it is a matter of inclination to avoid the influence of contextual information, hence the concept of Field Independence (Witkin, et al, 1974). In more general terms, FI is regarded as an inclination to analyze experiences. A person high on the FI extreme is said to seek differentiated information with well-distinguished parts. A person low on FI is less likely to analyze and is more influenced by contexts. The trait is not confined to visual information, but shows its effects with semantic and behavioral information as well. It is said to influence educational and vocational choices, and also approaches to learning (Witkin, 1976).

My interpretation of the FI trait is rather different. The cue for it comes from the fact that a Hidden Figures test (also based on the Gottschaldt figures) in a number of factor analyses has had significant loadings on the SI ability NVT (convergent production of visual transformations). The first conclusion might be that FI is to be identified with ability NVT. Although Witkin has on rare occasions spoken of FI as an ability, there are sufficient reasons for regarding it as not an ability and as not being as restricted in generality as SI ability NVT. Apparently, no one has reported a factor interpretable as an ability to analyze, and my own attempt to find such a factor failed (Wilson, Guilford, Christensen, & Lewis, 1954). Furthermore, there are the many other qualities that are reported to correlate with FI. The conclusion must be that the Hidden Figures test involves variances from both the trait of FI and the ability NVT.

Other tests of abilities also correlate with FI—tests that have in common some involvement with the SI product of transformation. As to SI operations, cognition and divergent-production tests have been found related (namely, tests for CVT and DVT). As to SI contents, tests of semantic and of behavioral information have also been found related. There is not enough information to say that all other content categories may be included also, but the product seems to be limited to transformation. The general conclusion seems to be that FI is a trait of flexibility in intellectual functioning—flexibility of the kind that depends upon transformations of information. It has not been disproven that FI, is, after all, a rather broad higher-order ability factor, nor has it been proven that it is a very general *set* to have transformations—in other words, a control trait. It is possible that there are two parallel broad traits, one an ability and one a control variable.

Complexity versus Simplicity. Another style that determines intellectual functioning is known as "Complexity versus Simplicity," to be noted hereafter as "Complexity." This trait has been demonstrated by means of classifying tasks. Typically, *S* is simply given a list of items of information and told to classify them in his own way, using as many or as few classes as he is inclined. A small number of classes is thought to indicate simple, broad conceptions and a large number to indicate complex conceptions.

The complexity or the simplicity pertains to the items that are classified, in other words, to units of information. The trait has been found to apply to tests in three kinds of SI contents—visual, semantic, and behavioral—since they have involved figures, words, and personalities to be classified. The operation seems to be cognition only.

A few investigators, such as Scott (1962), have also given *S* the option of reclassifying the units presented. Some *S*s show more reclassifications than others. This could indicate differences in the SI ability of DMC (divergent production of semantic classes) or, possibly in addition, an *attitude* of flexibility with regard to classes, another kind of control trait.

Equivalence Range. Equivalence Range (ER) is also concerned with broad versus narrow classes, but in a different way than is the trait of Complexity. Both are concerned with observations of similarities, but similarities of units exist in two different ways. One way is in terms of the proportions of attributes that pairs of units have in common. The other is in terms of the distance apart two units are on a scale or scales.

As usual, the nature of ER is indicated by the kinds of tests used for it. One form of test asks *S* to state estimates of what he regards to be the extreme values for given items on scales of measurement, having been told the average values. For example, the values might be for the length of whales, for the time it takes an ordinary man to run a distance of one kilometer, or for the heights of twelve-year-old girls in an ethnic group. The more extreme values *S* is inclined to give, the higher his position on the trait of ER.

A more definitive kind of test presents in turn a number of stimuli varying over a short range of values—some cards, for example, each having spots on it ranging in value near twenty in number. For each exposed card, *S* is to say whether or not the number is twenty. The more "yes" responses he gives, the greater his position on ER. Sorting tests have also been used. The items to be classified may be objects varying in size or figures differing in shape. All the described foregoing tests have positive intercorrelations, indicating a trait in common.

As to relations of ER to SI categories, since the tests call for judgments, the operation suggested is evaluation. Other ER tests, not mentioned, also look like evaluation tests. The tests call for evaluation of units or classes, more often classes. Three kinds of content have been used—visual, semantic, and behavioral. The identification of this trait with evaluation is further supported by the fact that some authors refer to the tests of it as being for "criticalness" or for "critical set."

Leveling versus Sharpening. The conception of a leveling-versus-sharpening dimension took its cue from some experiments by Gestalt psychologists on memory. It had been found that, with a lapse of time, remembered information tends to go in one of two directions: leveling or sharpening. Leveling smooths over rough or protruding features of figures, while sharpening tends to enhance or caricature notable features. The same contrasting tendencies also apply to stories as well as to figures. Individuals are inclined to go somewhat consistently in one direction or the other. A typical test of the trait presents material to be memorized then later applies recall tests on two different occasions. The experimenter examines the recalled material for changes in either direction.

So far as in known, the two trends apply only to visual and semantic information, with other kinds of content yet to be examined in this connection. The operation would seem obviously to be memory, but it is possible that the urge as to direction could be operating in cognition at the time of memorizing. The phenomena of leveling and sharpening suggest the question of whether the transformations are occurring during the period of retention or at the time of recall, or both. Such new problems are more likely to be generated when such findings are viewed in connection with the SI frame of reference.

Focusing versus Scanning. The style of Focusing versus Scanning (FS) is concerned with attention, as the terms would suggest. Attention is a matter of preparation for cognition, or for intellectual operations in general, rather than a *directional* control, as in other traits already mentioned. The bipolar FS dimension represents a range of behavior from a highly selective choice of information at the one extreme and a dispersion or roving of the spotlight of attention at the other. The FS dimension would possibly affect all aspects of intellectual functioning, but there would be some possible specializations along informational lines.

Analytical versus Global. The Analytical versus Global (AG) style also is a more general source of determination of intellectual events. Perhaps a better term than "analytical" would be the frequently used term "articulated." The latter extreme of the trait means a demand for sharpened discriminations, which could also be interpreted as an urge to gain more information, since information is dependent on discriminations. The globally oriented person is at ease without well-discriminated information.

In terms of SI categories, the operation is probably confined to cognition, but it could cut across all content, and possibly all product categories. The idea of possible lower-order AG traits—restricted to one or more of the SI informational categories—cannot be precluded. Individuals might more or less specialize their demands for clarity of information.

Intellectual Preferences

Some cognitive-style traits do have their determining influences on intellectual functioning, apparently, but by way of preferences rather than by direct control. The two or three traits last mentioned seem to be on the borderline in this respect. The styles to be discussed next are likely to have directional effects but with less compulsion. Such styles are also listed by Messick (1976). They have been less investigated, hence relations to the SI model are less certain, but definite hypotheses can be offered.

Messick speaks of a "Conceptual-styles" trait that concerns preferences in three directions: toward attributes (presumably SI units), toward classes, and toward relations. These variations are shown in tests calling for classifications of items of information. Some Ss tend to form classes with respect to attributes, some prefer to classify in terms of classes, and others stress relations as the basis for classification.

A trait called "Conceptualization" shows up in the form of rigidity with respect to class ideas; a disinclination to change classifications. Another proposed trait called "Conceptual Differentiation" seems to have the opposite characteristics. This suggests that actually the two styles are merely the opposite poles of the same dimension, and this dimension is connected with the SI category of abilities concerned with divergent production of classes. Its extensiveness among the SI content categories is yet to be determined.

The trait of "Integrative Complexity" involves a liking for dealing with multiple relations or categories. This description points to systems as the kind of product, and the modifier "multiple" suggests divergent production. In the semantic area this suggests the SI function of DMS. It might also suggest CMS.

There appear to be characteristic individual preferences among different categories of sensory information, namely among visual, auditory, and kinesthetic content categories. Another division of preferences among content categories is shown by preference for psychomotor activity versus conceptual activity. The SI content categories could be visual and kinesthetic on the one hand and semantic on the other. These content-preference affairs would suggest multiple dimensions of liking versus disliking for each kind of content mentioned.

A dichotomous type of preference situation seems also to apply in the case of two operation categories. Messick reports a style of preference for divergent versus convergent production. He describes the difference as a reliance on logical consistency—correct, conventional outcomes—versus the divergent pole of reliance on quantity and variety of output. In the author's own research (Guilford, Christensen, Frick, & Merrifield, 1961), a factor analysis of questionnaire items regarding liking for each of many kinds of thinking activity, two different factors were found in this immediate area, rather than one bipolar factor. The correlation between the scores for these two factors was about — .30, which does not confirm a bipolar factor but does show some negative relationship. The difference in findings may be explained by the fact that in the inventory approach, S is free to express liking or disliking for each item, but styles tests have probably called for forced-choice types of responses. The latter approach would force higher negative correlation. A higher-order bipolar factor, however would be a real possibility.

Other Personality Traits as Styles

There are still other cognitive styles that appear to be identifiable with personality traits of much broader scope. Their effects are not confined to intellectual functioning, but are broad enough to have effects among those functions, hence should be mentioned here. They are temperamental or motivational traits.

In discussing the style of "Scanning," Messick (1976) used the expressions "associated with meticulousness" and "concern for detail." Both descriptions fit the nature of the motivational factorial trait of "Meticulousness."[1] It can be suggested that the Risk-taking style, with its quality of willingness to take chances and to venture responses, could represent a combination of the factors of Self-confidence and Need for Adventure. A style described as a tolerance for unrealistic experiences or a readiness to accept unconventional ideas (also as little need to stay close to convention), seems near to the trait of Interest in Austistic Thinking.

Messick mentions a style of Reflection versus Impulsivity, which seems to have several possible affiliations with SI abilities as well as temperament traits. When he states that, in contrast with the reflective person, the impulsive person tends to give the first idea that occurs to him, he seems to be describing the temperament trait of Thoughtfulness in reverse. But possibly this style is identifiable with the second-order factor of introversion-extraversion, which rests upon the same trait plus the factor of Restraint (Guilford, 1977b). The possible connection with intellectual functioning is an inclination, or lack of it, to apply the operation of evaluation.

Messick also remarks that this style is concerned with the production of alternative hypotheses. This could easily describe the SI factor of DMI (divergent production of semantic implications). When he states further that there is also a testing of the hypotheses, he may be implying the parallel ability EMI. Some connection between these two abilities and Reflectiveness might be expected.

Discussion

From the foregoing review of the family of cognitive-style traits, it is clear that, although they have something to do with influencing

---

[1]For information concerning the traits of temperament and motivation mentioned here, see Guilford (1959a).

intellectual functioning in one way or another, they are by no means of the same kind of trait. The three general classes of such traits that were recognized in these presentations offer bases for discriminating among them. The styles differ with respect to whether there is more direct determining control over intellectual events, whether they are more in the form of interests or preferences, or they are personality traits of more general influence in behavior.

Another kind of variation that was pointed out in connection with many of the styles is in terms of logical connection with Structure-of-Intellect categories or functions. In most cases, the style traits cut across SI categories. The extent of this kind of generality is not fully known, owing to lack of investigations that would cover the whole SI model. Symbolic abilities, for example, and auditory content, were almost entirely missed in investigations of styles.

This feature of generality of styles raises the question of whether there might be higher-order factors of ability of parallel nature as to range of generality. The possibility of such aptitude factors has not been investigated to any appreciable extent, as yet. It is easy to agree with Messick (1973) when he proposes that higher-order ability factors should be expected to occur along the lines of the SI categories. Such an outcome would include possible factors at different levels of generality.

As yet there has been no evidence offered, to the effect that some of the styles are not higher-order abilities. For example, Field Independence might actually be a very general transformation ability. The styles that simply determine choices or show preferences seem definitely not to be abilities, nor do the temperamental and motivational traits.

The many apparent connections between style traits and SI abilities clearly suggest the value of using the SI model as a frame of reference in investigation of those traits. It even appears that individuals develop some naïve conceptions of the SI categories and that this helps to bring about the distinctions among the styles along SI lines. In a more general vein, in this survey of the cognitive styles we have additional support for the value of investigating individual differences in order to derive taxonomic conceptions of mental functioning.[2]

---

[2]For a fuller discussion of cognitive styles, see Guilford (1980) (in press).

Chapter 13
Some Further Considerations

In order to achieve some degree of closure to this volume, a few additional items must be mentioned. Although it is not claimed that the SI model, in its present form, can serve as a frame of reference for all kinds of mental events, there are some opportunities to extend its use beyond the intellectual domain. The extensions include some aspects of motivation and of emotional behavior. The least that can be said in this direction is that the same general approach of regarding behavior from the point of view of information processing can be more generally applied. That is what cognitive psychology should do.

There are also some more general implications of the SI model, and of the type of thinking that goes with it, in connection with certain aspects of intellectual functioning. Certain features of the model can suggest how the experimental investigator should proceed, whether he be of the bivariate or the multivariate persuasion. As to research outcomes, there are needs for operational models, based upon taxonomic models, as well as for additional taxonomic models. There are promising applications, which can only be touched upon, in connection with such special areas as speech, as well as with the technologies of education and psychotherapy.

A Discordant Note

Before proceeding futher, some attention must be given to a major criticism (Horn & Knapp, 1973) that has been made regarding the empirical basis for the SI model. Over the years of its existence, the Aptitudes Research Project (ARP) at the University of Southern California had rotated reference axes in its first analyses by the Zimmerman graphic method (Zimmerman, 1946) and in its later ones by the Cliff (1966) method of rotating all axes simultaneously toward hypothetically targeted factor structures. It had been found that rotations by any of the analytical methods that employ mathematically defined structures failed to give invariant results in terms of the same tests being significantly loaded on the same factors from one analysis to another. For the purpose of determining stable psychological variables, invariance of this type is demanded.

Horn and Knapp maintained that rotation toward almost any hypothetical, targeted factor matrix would ensure results close to that target. In order to test this idea, they selected three principal-axes matrices from the series of forty-one ARP analyses and set up for each one a target factor matrix that was generated by chance. Their claim was that their indices of goodness of fit of obtained matrix to target matrix were almost as good as for the fit obtained by the ARP approach.

In defense it can be said that the ARP matrix to which they gave most attention came from an analysis that had been done before the SI model had been developed, and the tests were not designed particularly in SI directions. That particular matrix was one of the most difficult ones from which to obtain a clear picture of psychological variables.

The most serious defect of the Horn-Knapp study was the fact that they used only one chance-generated target matrix in each rotational problem. The one that they used might, by chance, have been a very favorable one to support their thesis. That weakness was overcome by Elshout, Van Hemert, and Van Hemert (1975). They used not one chance-generated matrix but a large number for each analysis. The common result was that for each rotational problem there was a frequency distribution of indices of goodness of fit, and the index for the SI-targeted solution was way outside the entire frequency distribution of indices for the chance-generated targets.[1]

Some General Implications

Looking at the SI model as a whole, there are a number of further implications to be seen, some very general and others more specific.

The Brain as a Logical Device. One general conclusion is that, in whatever the human brain—that computer between our ears—does of an intellectual nature, it operates according to certain logical principles. The product of implication has recognized status in modern formal logic. The products of class and relation have logical overtones.

---

[1]For further information regarding these issues, see Guilford (1974, 1977c), Guilford & Hoepfner (1969), or Guilford & Zimmerman (1963).

The most complete justification for the stated generalization is to be seen in mathematics. Although the SI informational content involved in mathematics is confined to the symbolic and visual categories, all the kinds of products and all the kinds of operations do apply. Since the same operations and products apply in parallel fashion in the other content areas, it appears that mathematics provides an idealized picture of what happens in intellectual events in general. An important difference is that visual and symbolic items of information can be precisely defined. Although items in the other content areas are often poorly defined and incomplete, the brain seems to do the best it can under the circumstances, according to what is called a "psycho-logic" (Guilford, 1966). It may be said that formal logic was invented in order to make more rigorous evaluations of nonmathematical conclusions or implications. It is well known, of course, that semantically conceived problems are sometimes translated into mathematical terms in order to reach dependable answers. It would appear that mathematics, also, was invented to aid in reaching conclusions as well as in testing them. It can be claimed, then, that psycho-logic is more general than either formal logic or mathematics.

Further support for the psycho-logic view is found in instances in which the brain, in effect, seems to engage in quasi-mathematical performances. For example, Wooldridge (1963) has pointed out that even in the simple act of standing erect, in keeping bodily balance, the brain, in effect, solves differential equations. Examples of a statistical nature can also be cited. Individuals are known to form impressions of the probabilities of events and they gamble accordingly, as in the phenomenon of partial reinforcement. In forming what Helson (1964) called an adaptation level, the brain seems to be computing a weighted average of quantitative data. In classifying activities, it would appear that the individual is implicitly estimating a correlation coefficient in deciding on the degrees of similarities of pairs of items. One correlation coefficient—the G index of agreement (Holley & Guilford, 1964)—is a linear function of the proportion of attributes in common.

The Need for Operational Models

The Structure-of-Intellect model is sometimes characterized with the epithet of "static," which is an all-too-common way of dismissing ideas. But this is the nature of all taxonomic models, the chemists' periodic table being another example. Taxonomic models do not by themselves answer all the questions, but they lay important foundations for seeking further answers. We need good answers to the question "what" before we can do well in answering the question "how." In answering the second kind of question, operational models are very desirable for the psychologist. The latter type of model can be very usefully based on the former type. This approach has been demonstrated in my own problem-solving (SIPS) model, shown in Chapter 10, and in my model for behavior in general in Chapter 3. Under the influence of computer-simulation research and thinking, operational model building has gained some degree of popularity. Consideration of SI concepts should be useful in this connection.

Needs for SI Concepts in Experimental Research. The new SI concepts are very much needed in the research of both the bivariate experimental psychologist and the neurologist who is concerned with brain functioning. Many studies, particularly of the "higher mental processes," are inconclusive, even sometimes uninterpretable, because more precisely defined concepts were not employed. This is despite the fact that cognitive psychologists have somewhat generally taken to the employment of information-processing views of mental functioning.

In bivariate psychological experiments, as has been true of multivariate experiments, it would be very desirable to recognize that there are three major kinds of variation involved—operations, contents, and products—and to apply the appropriate controls where needed. Much too often this has not been done. For example, although there has been a recognition of the difference between verbal and nonverbal information in experiments on memory, much ambiguity remains. "Verbal" information could be either semantic or symbolic. It is true that the term "semantic memory" is beginning to appear in the literature. But there is further ambiguity with the "nonverbal" category. It could mean "visual," "auditory," or "symbolic." There is even the possibility that a distinction should be made between visual-symbolic and auditory-symbolic information.

Recognition of the kinds of SI abilities or functions can suggest the kinds of controls that should be applied in designing mental tasks for the experimental subjects, as had to be done in the multivariate experiments by way of factor analysis. In spite of such controls, the experimenter needs to be on the alert for miscarriages. Human subjects are often very resourceful. They may make translations from one code to another, or they make substitutions of SI products. However, such translations or transformations can sometimes be detected in a factor analysis. For example, in a study of memory abilities in a certain content area, it was found that some of the tests for remembering relations also had significant loadings on the factor for remembering transformations, and vice versa. This result could mean that many subjects were interpreting the printed before-and-after objects as presenting certain relations rather than transformations, and some were seeing intended transformations in the form of certain relations.

As for neurological research, it is already apparent, for example, that the different types of agnosias are clearly distinguished along the lines of SI abilities in the cognition category (Guilford, 1967). Where there is interest in determining correlations between psychological functions and brain functions or anatomy, it would be well for the investigator to describe mental functioning along SI lines. There are a few indications that this kind of study is becoming more common.

A Couple of Incidental Points

Other implications may seem at first thought to be of minor significance, but may deserve more than passing mention. One is that the SI model brings perception into the domain of intelligence, when the latter is as broadly conceived as it should be. Some more recently developed intelligence scales, such as the Wechsler and the Lorge-Thorndike, bring visual information prominently within the intellectual category, but in no case has it yet been recognized that the visual abilities are clearly parallel with the "verbal" abilities, nor is the semantic-symbolic distinction recognized. Behavioral information is still very much beyond the view of the intelligence tester. If there is any desire to measure a broad and balanced sampling of behavior by means of intelligence tests, there is much extending and balancing yet to be done.

From the standpoint of psychological theory, it should be added that the Gestalt psychologists did implicitly recognize the parallel events in different kinds of informational content. They very much favored research with visual information, assuming that what they found in that area would also apply in other areas, particularly semantic information. The two categories are indeed parallel, but not identical. Thus, although there should be many principles that apply in common, the investigator should be vigilant as to differences also, particularly in studies of memory.

One incidental point of curiosity about the SI model is that while two units of information involving the same kind of content in connection call for a relation as the connecting link (aside from cases of implications), three or more units in connection depend upon different abilities—those dealing with systems. This is true despite the fact that a system is composed of relations. the principle holds for all kinds of content. In the behavioral area, for example, two people seen interacting can well be used for an item for the ability CBR (cognition of behavioral relations), but three persons interacting provide an item for ability CBS. It is not yet clear what the significance of this two-versus-three variation may be. One could apply the

Gestalt dictum that the whole is more than the sum of its parts; a system is more than the relations that compose it. Or one could apply the old saying, in the behavioral area, at least, that two are company but three are a crowd.

An Informational View of Motivation

I have discussed some of the problems of motivation at length elsewhere (Guilford, 1965), and will only briefly summarize some of that thinking here. Despite the fact that motivation is concerned with ends in behavior, while intelligence would seem to be concerned with means to ends, it can be shown that, to a significant degree, certain aspects of the Structure of Intellect do apply to the understanding of many of its phenomena.

Phenomena of Motivation. We need to consider first the range of psychological events that come under the heading of motivation—phenomena that need to be accounted for by theory. It is generally recognized that the concept of "motivation" refers to a collection of mental events. For one thing, it is obvious that much behavior is spontaneous; it is generated from within the organism. An organism does not simply wait for externally imposed stimuli to initiate its actions. To a large extent it is self-starting, from internal sources.

Variations are also obvious in degree of effort or energy exhibited in actions. The amount of energy shown is not strongly dependent upon the amount in the stimulus. The organism performs at higher levels of activation at some times than at others, shown in terms of enthusiasm, speed, or power in its behavior.

Motives are also recognized as having directing influences. They determine where sense organs are directed and where energies are turned. In this connection there is sometimes talk of goals. Organisms do behave as if they are seeking certain environmental conditions or achievements. Since the days of the guided missile, it is less difficult for the scientific psychologist to speak of purposive behavior.

It is often recognized that environmental objects and events acquire motivational properties—the cathexes of Freud, the valences of Lewin, or the incentives of Hull. Both positive and negative incentives are taken into account—attractions and repulsions. The acquisition of values presents a number of problems.

Other aspects of behavior, including reinforcement, frustration, and conflict, bear rather direct relations to motivation. Most theories of learning give a prominent place to the phenomenon of reinforcement. What is the key to reinforcement? What happens when an organism is prevented from reaching its goal? What are the sources and consequences of conflicts? Such questions further indicate the importance of motivation.

An SI View of Motivation. In Chapter 5, in connection with learning, it was proposed that the secret of reinforcement is to be found in the SI operation of evaluation. The learner, a confirmed pragmatist, often with the aid of available feedback information, judges whether or not his responses are correct, suitable, or desirable. This view is sufficiently general to include all the suggested keys to reinforcement: Thorndike's pleasure and pain (in his law of effect), Hull's drive reduction, knowledge of results, and Thorndike's "confirming reaction." Any of these events can serve as "stop" and "go" signals for actions when the organism is again presented with the same situation or a similar one.

The last two suggested interpretations more clearly place reinforcement in the realm of intellectual activity, involving the operation of evaluation of information in all the SI content areas and in all of the product categories. The suggestions of pleasure and pain and of drive reduction point to the category of behavioral information of the self-generated variety.

This line of thinking leads us to the recognition that we cognize not only our own feelings but also our own drive states. This statement does not commit us to a belief that we know all our drives consciously. But it does open the way to the belief that some cognitions can be unconscious. The latter statement does not entail the animistic concept of an unconscious mind. It is possible, of course, that internally generated information is just poorly structured, since in the course of the development of the individual there is a lack of feedback information that would help in gaining more refined structuring, such as occurs with input from exteroceptors. Furthermore, the individual can function passably without that refinement.

Cognition of drive status can include information regarding the degree of vitalness or urgency of the situation, and thus can regulate the amount of energy mobilized and released to meet the situation. Goals are commonly behavioral implications that have been learned in connection with motives and that are anticipated more or less clearly by the individual. Objects and events become valued in terms of anticipated states of well-being or ill-being. Thus, many of the phenomena of motivation can be interpreted in terms of information processing, and more specifically, as cognition of implications.

In this connection it is significant that factor-analytic investigations of the ability known provisionally as "sensitivity to problems" turned out to be in the SI area of cognition of implications. When an individual sees that a problem exists, he becomes aware that certain things are not as they should be. Determining the nature of the problem calls for further cognitive activity. Work toward solution of the problem is motivated by anticipated changes in the situation that caused it.

Toward Taxonomies of Feelings and Emotions

Like motives, experienced feelings and emotions can be regarded as self-generated behavioral information. They occur as implications from other cognized items of information. This statement is becoming recognized as applying in connection with autonomic reactions. After years of research, and a thorough review of the literature, Grings (1973) came to the conclusion that "conscious awareness determines autonomic behavior." In the case of the conditioned galvanic skin response, for example, he has concluded that a stimulus serves as a signal for a significant impending event. This expectation is an implication. From another literature survey, Ryan (1970) came to the same kind of conclusion.

A Taxonomy of Feelings. A taxonomic model for feelings came about rather indirectly from what were actually regarded as investigations of meaning. Osgood, Suci, and Tannenbaum (1957) applied an ingenious method, which involved factor analysis, to the meanings of words. Each of a list of words was rated with respect to a list of attributes by a number of subjects, following which the words were intercorrelated and the intercorrelations factor analyzed. Three strong, verifiable factors were found and were interpreted as being for the dimensions of *value* (good-bad), *activity* (active-passive), and *power* (strong-weak). Osgood, Suci, and Tannenbaum proposed describing the meanings of words in terms of their positions on the three factorial dimensions.

It must be realized, however, that such a description of the meaning of a word is usually far from complete. The meaning of a word, in SI interpretation, is a semantic unit. Elsewhere, I have presented a theory of the meaning of a semantic unit that regards it as a pattern of implied information (Guilford, 1967). That is, the meaning of any word is everything that it implies for the individual who uses it—a collection of connected attributes. Among these attributes can be feelings, but they are mostly in the connotative aspect of the meaning and not in the denotative aspect, which actually defines the word. Thus, the Osgood taxonomy of feeling is an empirical demonstration of Wundt's tri-dimentional theory of feeling.

Some Taxonomic Concepts of Emotions. There have been some efforts to achieve relatively independent, dimensional concepts in the domain of emotions. Some efforts have been through the factor analysis of individual differences in moods (Nowlis & Nowlis, 1956; Borgatta, 1961; Green, 1965). Moods, which have been regarded as determiners of behavior, were broadly defined as "frames of mind" or temporary dispositions. A different kind of attempt to find dimensions of emotion applied scaling methods to facial expressions, as reported by Wood-worth and Schlossberg (1954).

In the studies of moods the data were in the form of self-reported descriptions, using adjectives, which were factor-analyzed. The Nowlis-Green list of mood factors included the following qualities: Aggression, Social Affection, Surgency, Elation, Sadness, Vigor, Fatigue, Anxiety, Concentration, Egotism, and Skepticism. From the names of these dimensions, it is fairly clear that the involvement of emotion varies—that there are non-emotional aspects to many of them. Measures of these mood factors have been recommended for use in studies of the effects of different personal conditions on moods—conditions such as drug states, working, and boredom—and in studies of the effects of moods on responses.

In my book *Personality* (1959a), the basic axiom proposed for behavior is that in addition to stimulus situations, behavior is determined by internal or organismic features, including temporary personal conditions and more permanent dispositions or personality traits. Moods come within the temporary-condition category, since they change from time to time. But the naming of the moods, as just indicated, raises some question as to whether they are all within the temporary category or whether some of them, at least, should be identified as enduring traits. The operational difference is that traits are made evident in individual cases by asking the person how he feels or acts over the general run of experiences, whereas moods are assessed by asking the subject to focus on the current moment.

Some parallels between moods and traits can be noted. Corresponding to the mood of Aggression there is the factorial trait of Aggressiveness. For the mood of Concentration there is the very similar trait of Thoughtfulness. Surgency is described like the trait of Rhathymia. Vigor goes with the factorial trait of General Activity. There are some other resemblances, but not on a one-to-one basis. One good hypothesis is that the personality traits that have clearly parallel characteristics undergo unusual degrees of functional fluctuations, which permits the individual to exhibit temporarily varying positions on their scales.

The dimensions of emotions thought to have been obtained from the studies of facial expressions were identified as P-U (pleasant-unpleasant) and A-R (attention-rejection). The former could be readily identified with the affective or feeling factorial dimension found from a quite different approach by Osgood, Suci, and Tannenbaum (1957). The latter trait raises some logical questions. Attention and rejection are not logical opposites. It would seem, instead, that they refer to two different dimensions: attention-inattention and acceptance-rejection. An approach through factor analysis might produce such a separation.

Dimensions of Other Domains. A complete cognitive psychology should be expected to take into account all traits of personality as determiners of behavior. The chapters of this volume have been mainly restricted to traits in the areas of intellectual abilities and cognitive styles. More extensive efforts toward systematizing the findings of multivariate analyses, although more modestly proposed as a theory of individuality, have been reported by Royce (1973). Royce chose to apply the hierarchical model throughout to trait interrelationships. To a large extent this kind of effort is premature due to lack of adequate information regarding the primary traits in some areas, and especially regarding interrelationships.

To mention another area that may be subjected to multivariate research, Sells (1973) makes the novel but reasonable suggestion that psychologists should attempt to determine significant dimensions of environments. There should be descriptive variables regarding situations as well as those describing behavior. Sell's proposal may be pointing to a seriously neglected area of investigation and to a potentially profitable one.

SI Functions in Speech

Some specialists in the field of speech have noted the applicability of SI concepts to that area of behavior. The extensiveness of the applications is indicated by Wiig and Semel (1976), for example, in their studies of language disabilities. From their accounts of special speech difficulties in children, the following list of connections can be pointed out. Each SI function that is concerned is stated, with examples of deficiencies.[1]

CAU - Difficulty in forming a spoken word.
CMU - Difficulty in forming new concepts, especially abstract ones.
 - Difficulty in following directions.
 - Focusing on some attributes to the neglect of others.
 - Knowing only one use for an object.
CMC - Failure to put new words in a class.
 - Failure to exclude words that do not belong in a class.
CVR - Some confusion regarding the spatial order of two things.
CMR - Failure to grasp analogies.
 - Some confusion regarding the temporal order of two things.
CMS - Failure to understand problems.

---

[1]This author is willing to assume responsibility for the given SI identifications. Trigram labels for functions are used to save space. For translations of trigrams, see the Appendix.

            - Difficulty in reading complex material.
CMT   - Inability to redefine words.
            - Inability to use same word in new contexts.
CMI   - Given the beginning of a story, inability to finish it.
            - Inability to grasp what is only suggested, such as in
              fables, parables or proverbs.
CBU   - Low in social perception (emotions and attitudes, for
              example).
DMU   - Inability to name class members, given a class name.
DMS   - Limited flexibility in forming systems.
            - Restriction to simple, declarative sentences.
NMU   - Slow and inacurate naming of objects, events, or
              opposites (the greater the restriction in naming,
              the greater the difficulty).
EMU   - Using a verb with the wrong tense.
            - Using incorrect prepositions.
            - Inconsistencies within the same sentences.

There are undoubtedly more such identifications. For example, there are difficulties with syntax, some of which may involve symbolic items of information. There are probably many additional defects dependent upon auditory inabilities.

The Structure of Intellect and Education

The relations of SI concepts to education have been treated with some elaboration elsewhere (Guilford, 1977d; 1978). Only some of the high points will be given attention here. For some of the information on this subject, references can be made to earlier chapters in this volume.

Learning in Education. Education's prime responsibility, of course, is the learning to be achieved by its clients. Probably the most pervasive contribution that SI concepts can make, therefore, is the somewhat revolutionary conception of learning. The statement is made in this fashion because the view is definitely more comprehensive than the associative doctrine that has been dominant for so many years. There should be some reservations, however, for teachers have actually not been self-restricted to the teaching of associations. It should also be noted that Gestalt psychologists vigorously attacked the associative view and proposed an alternative that is fundamentally like the SI position.

As suggested in Chapter 5, learning is defined as the construction of new items of information; items of any of the six kinds of products in any category of content. An association, being an SI implication, is only one of the six kinds. The items are structured by the learner's brain. If an item should fall into place rather suddenly, in an unusually large step, the term "insight" is sometimes applied. The structuring, or coding, is the SI operation of cognition. Since the total act of learning includes putting new items of information into storage, the SI operation of memory is also involved. The teacher should recognize what kind of item is to be learned and should possess the procedures that assist learners to make the proper constructions. Learners, also, can profit by knowing what kinds of items must be formed.

One of the special problems of teaching and learning—reinforcement—is, as indicated earlier, a matter of the SI operation of evaluation, with the aid of feedback information. The role of repetition in learning is its provision of renewed opportunities for shaping or reshaping items of information. The new interpretation of transfer of learning is in terms of the number of attributes in common, including the SI categories. The maximum opportunity for positive transfer occurs when all three aspects are in common—operation, content, and product. Avoidance of negative transfer and of interference is to be found in increased precision of items of information.

Educating for Intelligence. As just indicated, one side of the educational coin is concerned with the uses of knowledge concerning the Structure of Intellect in the promotion of learning in the educational milieu. The other side concerns the possibilities of improving SI abilities through the processes of education. First to be considered is the extent to which SI functions are exercised through the normal practices of education. In making a survey of any educational regimen in the search for an answer to this question, the SI model can serve well as the frame of reference.

When this approach has been applied, it has been found that, of the SI operations, cognition and memory are relatively overemphasized, with relative lack of attention to the categories of productive thinking and of evaluation (Aschner, 1963). This finding is only natural, in that cognition and memory are fundamental and necessary. But too often teachers think their tasks are done when this much is achieved. This much activity serves to stock the memory stores of students, but it does not contribute sufficiently to skills in programming—in the use of stored information. Knowledge must also be made functional.

Imbalances involving content and product categories have not been similarly investigated, but it is likely that semantic functions are given the most exercise, since all instruction involves communication, and behavioral functions receive the least, at least formally. Of the products, units and systems probably receive the greatest amount of attention, and transformations the least. The probable slighting of both divergent production and transformations would mean that preparation for creative thinking is slighted, to say the least.

Incidentally, the imbalances in education are paralleled by similar imbalances in tests of intelligence. This situation is understandable, since the first, and subsequent, intelligence tests were designed for the purpose of predicting which children should be expected to advance normally in school. In connection with the objective of improving intellectual functions through the normal course of instruction, there are needs to consider curriculum, teacher behavior, and examinations, and their probable values in meeting the objective.

A much more direct approach is to give the learners special exercises in SI functions. The exercises can be of the kinds of tasks that have been used in tests for demonstrating the SI abilities. A number of schools in Japan and in the United States have adopted this route, with reports of demonstrated positive results. An International Society for Intelligence Education has been formed, to facilitate this type of approach in education. Children who have learning difficulties in the usual course work are assessed with tests of selected SI abilities in an attempt to pinpoint the trouble in terms of one or more weak abilities. Special exercises are given in order to build up the weak functions. If that should fail, the child's stronger abilities are determined and, as much as possible, teaching is directed through those avenues.

Education for Intellectual Control. As proposed in the preceding Chapter, many of the traits known as "cognitive styles" are in the form of different kinds of controls of intellectual functioning, and their effects are directed along the lines of the SI categories. It is not yet clear just where efforts to develop desirable controls should be directed or the kinds of benefits to be derived. One step toward facilitating development of those controls would be to teach learners about the nature of their various intellectual resources, and where and how to turn them on and off, thus increasing personal management of those resources. The "intellectual executive functions" could thus be developed and utilized.

Incidentally, the proposed "motor executive functions," if further research bears out the predictive projection of such a category, could be very useful concepts in connection with any learned psychomotor skills—handwriting, musical performance, physical education, and athletics. In this executive area, especially, further research is badly needed. For such areas taxonomies for intentional behavior would seem to be within the realm of possibility.

SI and Mental Health

Of the many varieties of psychotherapy, certain ones adopt more rational approaches, realizing that the basic troubles are that patients have problems to be solved. Such approaches are likely to emphasize intellectual functioning, as is perhaps best illustrated by the views of Mahoney (1974, 1977) and of Torrance (1965), whose book on the subject contains a wealth of information that makes use of Structure-of-Intellect concepts, in constructive ways.

According to Torrance's view, mental health means responding constructively to stress. Healthy personalities are achieved by developing skills for dealing with stress. There is a two-way relation between personal failure and stress. On the one hand, intellectual failures can be causes of stress, sometimes severe stress. On the other hand, unusual stress can cause failures in any of the SI functions. There is misinterpretation of situations (cognition); forgetting of critical items of information; poverty of generated ideas to meet problems (divergent production); arrival at wrong conclusions (convergent production); and poor judgments, leading to poor decisions (evaluation). In an overanxious condition there is a lack of goals; there is a distractive tie-up of energies; there may be conformity for conformity's sake, and disconformity for disconformity's sake. Habits of coping with stress must be developed, and the approach is through intellectual operations. Failure to develop such habits may, in some cases, lead to neuroses or psychoses.

More specifically Torrance explains the roles of SI operations in coping with stress, and their relations to mental health. He points out problems that arise, reasons for failures, some other personality traits that may be related, and how the SI operations are affected by social conditions. Numerous suggestions are made for improving the SI functions, with special procedures for development.

Reports from scattered sources tend to bear out Torrance's proposed treatments through improving intellectual abilities. Where special efforts have been made to develop certain SI abilities, particularly those in the area of divergent production, a commonly reported effect is that the children's general attitudes are improved. They have more self-respect and more self-confidence. Children whose learning difficulties have been remedied by special SI development have improved attitude toward school, and some behavior problems may have been solved. Apparently there is general relief from frustration.

Remaining Taxonomic Problems

Perhaps the best way of concluding this volume is to point out some work remaining to be done in the way of deriving taxonomic psychological concepts. As matters now stand, parts of the Structure-of-Intellect model still need empirical evidence, and models are needed for other areas of functioning.

The largest segment of the SI model needing attention is in the auditory-content area. Only about a half-dozen abilities or functions of that nature have been demonstrated. A whole column has been projected, however, because the few known auditory abilities seem clearly parallel with those in the visual and other content categories. Such functions should be of greatest importance in speech and in music, and in other activities that depend upon them. A whole content area for kinesthetic information should be considered for addition to the SI model.

The next largest category needing attention is that of behavioral information. The abilities for behavioral cognition and for behavioral divergent production have been accounted for, but functions of behavioral memory, convergent production, and evaluation remain. These convergent-production abilities should be significant in the areas of ethical and legal conclusions. The corresponding evaluation functions should be relevant to ethical and legal judgments and decisions.

A very good beginning seems to have been made in discovering executive functions that operate in the voluntary control of intellectual activity, functions commonly known as cognitive styles. There is just a hint that there may be a whole family of executive functions concerned with the control of motor activity. An example of such a function is in connection with the disorder of aphasia. It may reflect a loss in a particular executive function (or functions) in the area of speech.

The limited excursions into dimensional analyses of feelings and emotions are another indication of the potential fruitfulness of seeking taxonomic concepts by way of experimental multivariate analyses. The investigator by this route should be warned, however, that following orthodox factor-analytic procedures religiously may lead to failure. Only when there has been a nearly ideal selection of experimental variables for the analysis will such steps yield consistent psychological pictures. Only well-planned analyses lead to success; advice that is in line with that of Thurstone from early in his presentation of his method of multiple factor analysis.

Appendix

Code to Structure-of-Intellect Trigrams

In each trigram symbol for a Structure-of-Intellect ability or function, the first letter stands for the kind of operation involved, the second letter for the kind of informational content, and the third for the kind of product, as associated in the following lists:

Operation		Content		Product	
C	cognition	V	visual	U	unit
M	memory	A	auditory	C	class
D	divergent production	S	symbolic	R	relation
N	convergent production	M	semantic	S	system
E	evaluation	B	behavioral	T	transformation
				I	implication

Examples: CVT - cognition of visual transformations
MMI - memory for semantic implications
DBS - divergent production of behavioral systems
NSC - convergent production of symbolic classes
EAU - evaluation of auditory units

References

Allen, M. S., Guilford, J. P., & Merrifield, P. R. The evaluation of selected intellectual factors by creative research scientists. *Reports from the Psychological Laboratory,* no. 25. Los Angeles: University of Southern California, 1960.

Arib, M. A. Cognition—A cybernetic approach. In P. L. Garvin (ed.), *Cognition: A multiple view.* New York: Spartan Books, 1970. Pp. 331-348.

Aschner, M. J. The analysis of verbal interaction in the classroom. In A. Bellack (ed.), *Theory and research in teaching.* New York: Teachers College Publications, 1963.

Barnard, C. J. *The function of the executive.* Cambridge, Mass.: Harvard University Press, 1938.

Bartlett, M. S. The statistical conception of mental factors. *British Journal of Psychology,* 1937, 28, 97-108.

Berger, R. M., Guilford, J. P., & Christensen, P. R. A factor-analytic study of planning. *Psychological Monographs,* 1957, no. 71 (whole no. 435).

Borgatta, E. F. Mood, personality, and interaction. *Journal of General Psychology,* 1961, 64, 105-137.

Boring, E. G. *A history of experimental psychology, 2d ed. New York: Appleton-Century-Crofts, 1950.*

Broadbent, *D.E. Perception and Communication.* New York: Pergamon, 1958.

Broadbent, D. E. Flow of information within the organism. *Journal of Verbal Learning and Verbal Behavior,* 1963, 2, 24-39.

Broverman, D. M. Cognitive style and intraindividual variation in abilities, *Journal of Personality,* 1960, 28, 240-256.

Brown, S. W., Guilford, J. P., & Hoepfner, R. Six semantic-memory abilities. *Educational and Psychological Measurement,* 1968, 28, 691-717.

Burt, C. The structure of mind: A review of the results of factor analysis. *British Journal of Psychology,* 1949, 19, 100-111, 176-199.

Bush, R. R., & Mosteller, F. *Stochastic models for learning.* New York: Wiley, 1955.

Capra, F. *The Tao of physics.* San Francisco: Shambahala Press, 1975.

Cattell, R. B. *Personality and motivation structure and measurement.* Yonkers: World Book Company, 1957.

Chorness, M. H. The effects of multivariate selection and mild stress upon complex problem solving and creative thinking. Doctoral dissertation, University of Texas, 1959.

Cliff, N. Orthogonal rotation to congruence. *Psychometrika,* 1966, 31, 33-42.

Cline, V.B., Richards, J.M. Jr., & Abe, C. The validity of a battery of creativity tests in a high school sample. *Educational and Psychological Measurement,* 1962, 22, 781-784.

Cohen, J. *Behavior in uncertainty.* London: Allen & Unwin, 1964.

Cohen, J., & Hansel, C. E. M. *Risk and gambling: The study of subjective probability.* London: Longmans Green, 1956.

Cohen, J., & Hansel, C. E. M. Subjective probability, gambling, and intelligence. *Nature,* 1958, 181, 1150-1161.

Cronbach, L. J. The two disciplines of scientific psychology. *American Psychologist,* 1957, 12, 671-684.

Crossman, E. R. F. W. Information processing in human skills, *British Medical Bulletin,* 1964, 20, 32-37.

Dewey, J. *How we think.* Boston: D. C. Heath, 1933.

Dunham, J. L., Guilford, J. P., & Hoepfner, R. Abilities pertaining to classes and the learning of concepts. *Reports from the Psychological Laboratory,* no. 39. Los Angeles: University of Southern California, 1966.

Dunham, J. L., Guilford, J. P., & Hoepfner, R. Multivariate approaches to discovering the intellectual components of concept learning. *Psychological Review,* 1968, 75, 206-221.

Edwards, W. The theory of decision making. *Psychological Bulletin,* 1954, 51, 380-417.

Edwards, W. Behavioral decision theory. In P.R. Farnsworth (ed.), Annual Reviews of Psychology. Palo Alto, CA.: Annual Reviews, 1961, 12, 473-498.

Elshout, J. J., Van Hemert, N. A., & Van Hemert, M. Comment on the subjective character of the empirical basis of Guilford's

Structure-of-Intellect model. *Tijdschrift Onderwijsearch,* 1975, 1, 15-25.

Estes, W. K. Toward a statistical theory of learning. *Psychological Review,* 1950, 57, 94-107.

Eysenck, H.J. & Eysenck, S.B.G. *Personality structure and measurement.* San Diego: Knapp, 1969.

Feldman, B. Prediction of first-grade reading achievement from selected Structure-of-Intellect factors. Doctoral dissertation, University of Southern California, 1967.

Ferguson, G. A. On learning and known abilities. *Canadian Journal of Psychology,* 1954, 8, 95-112.

Ferguson, G. A. On transfer and abilities of man. *Canadian Journal of Psychology,* 1956, 10, 121-131.

Fleishman, E. A. *Individual differences in motor learning.* Washington D. C.: American Institutes for Research, 1966.

Fleishman, E.A., & Hempel, W.E., Jr. Changes in factor structure of a complex psychomotor test as a function of practice. *Psychometrika,* 1954, 19, 239-252.

Fleishman, E. A., & Hempel W. E., Jr. The relation between abilities and improvement with practice in a visual discrimination reaction time task. *Journal of Experimental Psychology,* 1955, 49, 301-312.

Frick, J. W., Guilford, J. P., Christensen, P. R., & Merrifield, P. R. A factor-analytic study of flexibility of thinking. *Educational and Psychological Measurement,* 1959, 19, 469-496.

Garner, W. R., *Uncertainty and structure as psychological concepts.* New York: Wiley, 1962.

Garvin, P. L. *Cognition: A multiple view.* New York: Spartan Books, 1970.

Getzels, J. W., & Jackson, P. W. *Creativity and intelligence.* New York: Wiley, 1961.

Green, R. F. *On the measurement of mood.* Technical Report No. 10, Research Project NR 171-342, Contract No. Nonr-66C (12), 1965.

Green, R. F., Guilford, J. P. Christensen, P. R., & Comrey, A. L. A factor-analytic study of reasoning abilities. *Psychometrika,* 1953, 135-160.

Grings, W. W. The role of consciousness and cognition in autonomic behavior changes. In F. J. McQuigan & R. A. Schoonover, *The psychophysiology of thinking.* New York: Academic Press, 1973.

Guilford, J. P. Creativity. *American Psychologist,* 1950, 5, 444-454.

Guilford, J. P. The structure of intellect. *Psychological Bulletin,* 1956, 53, 267-293.

Guilford, J. P. A system of psychomotor abilities. *American Journal of Psychology,* 1958, 71, 164-174.

Guilford, J. P. *Personality.* New York: McGraw-Hill, 1959. a

Guilford, J. P. Three faces of intellect. *American Psychologist,* 1959, 14, 469-479. b

Guilford, J. P. Basic conceptual problems in the psychology of thinking. In E. Harms (ed.), Fundamentals of the psychology of thinking. *Annals of the New York Academy of Sciences,* 1960, 91, 6-21. a

Guilford, J. P. An emerging view of learning theory, In J. A. Ross & R. Thompson (eds.), *Proceedings of the 1960 Summer Conference.* Bellingham, Wash.: Western Washington College, 1960, Pp. 29-48. b

Guilford, J. P. Factorial angles to psychology. *Psychological Review,* 1961, 68, 1-20.

Guilford, J.P. Motivation in an informational psychology. In D. Levin (ed.), *Nebraska symposium on motivation, 1965.* Lincoln, Neb.: University of Nebraska Press, 1965. Pp. 313-332.

Guilford, J. P. Intelligence: 1965 model. *American Psychologist,* 1966, 21, 20-26.

Guilford, J. P. *The nature of human intelligence.* New York: McGraw-Hill, 1967.

Guilford, J. P. Intelligence has three facets. *Science,* 1968, 160, 615-620.

Guilford, J. P. Varieties of memory and their implications. *Journal of General Psychology,* 1971, 85, 207-228.

Guilford, J. P. Executive functions and a model of behavior. *Journal of General Psychology,* 1972, 86, 279-287.

Guilford, J.P. Theoretical issues and operational-informational psychology. In J. R. Royce (ed.), *Contributions of multivariate analysis to psychological theory.* London: Academic Press, 1973. Pp. 241-262.

Guilford, J. P. Rotation problems in factor analysis. *Psychological Bulletin,* 1974, 81, 498-501.

Guilford, J.P. Factors and factors of personality. *Psychological Bulletin,* 1975, 83, 802-814.

Guilford, J. P. *Way beyond the IQ: Guide to improving intelligence and creativity.* Buffalo: Creative Education Foundation, 1977 a

Guilford, J. P. Will the real factor of extraversion-introversion please stand up? A reply to Eysenck. *Psychological Bulletin,* 1977, 84, 412-416. b

Guilford, J. P. The invariance problem in factor analysis. *Educational and Psychological Measurement,* 1977, 37, 11-19. c

Guilford, J. P. Education with an informational psychology. *Education,* 1977, 98, 3-16. d

Guilford, J.P. Intelligence isn't what it used to be: What to do about it. *Journal of Research and Development in Education.* 11, 1978 (In Press)

Guilford, J.P. Cognitive styles: What are they? *Educational and Psychological Measurement.* 40, 1980 (In Press)

Guilford, J. P., Christensen, P. R. Frick, J. W., & Merrifield, P. R. Factors of interest in thinking. *Journal of General Psychology,* 1961, 65, 39-56.

Guilford, J. P., Dunham, J. L., & Hoepfner, R. Roles of intellectual abilities in the learning of concepts. *Proceedings of the National Academy of Sciences,* 1967, 58, 1812-1817.

Guilford, J.P., & Hoepfner, R. Comparison of varimax rotations with rotations to theoretical targets. *Educational and Psychological Measurement,* 1969, 29, 3-22.

Guilford, J. P. & Hoepfner, R. *The analysis of intelligence.* New York: McGraw-Hill, 1971.

Guilford, J. P. & Lacey, J. I. *Printed classification tests: Army Air Forces Aviation Psychology Research Program Reports,* Report No. 5. Washington D. C.: U. S. Government Printing Office, 1947.

Guilford, J. P., & Zimmerman, W. S. *The Guilford-Zimmerman Aptitude Survey.* Beverly Hills, Calif.: Sheridan Supply Co., 1956.

Guilford, J. P., & Zimmerman, W. S. Some variable-sampling problems in the rotation of axes in factor analysis. *Psychological Bulletin,* 1963, 60, 289-301.

Guthrie, E. R. *The psychology of learning.* New York: Harper, 1952.

Guttman, L. A new approach to factor analysis: The radex. In P. F. Lazersfeld (ed.), *Mathematical thinking in the social sciences.* Glencoe, Ill.: Free Press, 1954.

Helson, H. The psychology of Gestalt. *American Journal of Psychology,* 1925, 36, 342-370, 494-526; 1926, 37, 25-32, 169-223.

Hendricks, M., Guilford, J.P., & Hoepfner, R. Measuring creative social intelligence. *Reports from the Psychological Laboratory,* no. 42. Los Angeles: University of Southern California, 1969.

Hoepfner, R., & Guilford, J. P. Sixteen divergent-production abilities at the ninth-grade level. *Multivariate Behavioral Research,* 1966, 1, 43-66.

Hoepfner, R., Guilford, J. P., & Bradley, P. A. Transformation of information in learning. *Journal of Educational Psychology,* 1970, 61, 316-323.

Holley, J. W., & Guilford, J. P. A note on the G index of agreement. *Educational and Psychological Measurement,* 1964, 24, 749-754.

Horn, J. L., & Knapp, J. R. On the subjective character of the empirical basis for Guilford's Structure-of-Intellect model. *Psychological Bulletin,* 1973, 80, 33-43.

Hull, C. L. *Principles of behavior.* New York: Appleton-Century-Crofts, 1952.

Hunt, E. B. *Artificial intelligence.* New York: Academic Press, 1975.

Kamstra, O. W. M. *De dimensionaliteit van het geheugen. Ein Faktor-analitisch anderzoek.* Amsterdam: Van Soext, 1971.

Karlin, J. E. Music ability. *Psychometrika,* 1941, 6, 61-65.

Katzenberger, L. *Dimensionen des Gedachtnisses: Eine empirische Untersuchungen ueber die faktorielle Structure der Gedächtnis Fahigkeit.* Würzburg: Bamberg, 1964.

Kettner, N. W., Guilford, J. P., & Christensen, P. R. A factor-analytic study across the domains of reasoning, creativity, and evaluation. *Psychological Monographs,* 1959, 73, no. 9 (whole no. 479).

Kluever, R.C. A study of Guilford's memory factors in normal and children with reading disabilities. Doctoral dissertation, Northwestern University, 1968.

Kogan, N., & Wallach, M. A. *Risk taking: A study of cognition and personality.* New York: Rinehart & Winston, 1964.

Köhler, W. On the nature of association. *Proceedings of the American Philosophical Society,* 1941, 84, 489-502.

Lazersfeld, P. F. A conceptual introduction to latent structure analysis. In P. F. Lazersfeld (ed.), *Mathematical thinking in the social sciences.* Glencoe, Ill.: Free Press, 1954.

Luce, R. D. *Individual chance behavior.* New York: Wiley, 1959.

Luce, R. D., & Raiffa, H. *Games and decisions.* New York: Wiley, 1957.

Mahoney, M. J. *Cognition and behavior modification.* Cambridge, Mass.: Ballinger, 1974.

Mahoney, M. J. Reflections on the cognitive learning trend in psychotherapy. *American Psychologist,* 1977, 32, 5-13.

Meeker, M. N. *The structure of intellect: Its interpretation and uses.* Columbus, Ohio: Merrill, 1969.

Merrifield, P. R., Guilford, J. P., Christensen, P. R., & Frick, J. W. A factor-analytic study of problem-solving abilities. *Reports from the Psychological Laboratory,* no. 22. Los Angeles: University of Southern California, 1960.

Messick, S. Multivariate models of cognition and personality: The need for both process and structure in psychological theory and measurement. In J.R. Royce (ed.), *Multivariate analysis and psychological theory.* New York: Academic Press, 1973. Pp. 265-303.

Messick, S. Personality consistencies in cognition and creativity. In S. Messick (ed.), *Individuality in learning.* San Francisco: Jossey-Bass, 1976. Pp. 4-33.

Miller, G. A., Galanter, E., & Pribram, K. H. *Plans and the structure of behavior.* New York: Holt, 1960.

Mowrer, O. H. *Learning theory and behavior.* New York: Wiley, 1960.

Neisser, U. *Cognitive psychology.* Englewood Cliffs, N. J.: Prentice-Hall, 1967.

Newel, A., Shaw, J.C., & Simon, H.A. Elements of a theory of human problem solving. *Psychological review,* 1958, 65, 151-166.

Nowlis, V., & Nowlis, H. H. the description and analysis of mood. *Annals of the New York Academy of Sciences,* 1956, 65, 345-355.

Osgood, C. E., Suci, G. J., & Tannenbaum, P. H. *The measurement of meaning.* Urbana, Ill.: University of Illinois Press, 1957.

Rossman, J. *The psychology of the inventor.* Washington, D.C.: Inventors Publishing Company, 1931.

Royce, J. R. The conceptual framework for a multi-factor theory of individuality. In J. R. Royce (ed.), *Multivariate analysis and psychological theory.* New York: Academic Press, 1973. Pp. 305-381.

Ryan, T. A. *Intentional behavior.* New York: Ronald Press, 1970.

Santostefano, S. Cognitive controls versus styles: Diagnosing and treating cognitive disabilities in children. *Seminars in Psychiatry,* 1969, 1, 281-317.

Savage, L. J. *The foundations of statistics.* New York: Wiley, 1954.

Scott, W. A. Cognitive complexity and cognitive flexibility. *Sociometry,* 1962, 25, 405-414.

Sells, S. B. Prescriptions of a multivariate model in personality and psychological theory: Ecological considerations. In J. R. Royce (ed.), *Multivariate analysis and psychological theory.* New York: Academic Press, 1973. Pp. 103-108.

Simon, H. A. *Administrative behavior.* New York: Macmillan, 1947.

Simon, H. A. *Models of man.* New York: Wiley, 1957.

Skinner, B. F. Are theories of learning necessary? *Psychological Review,* 1950, 57, 193-216.

Spearman, C. "General intelligence," objectively determined and measured. *American Journal of Psychology,* 1904, 15, 201-293.

Spearman, C. *The nature of "intelligence" and principles of cognition.* New York: Macmillan, 1923.

Spearman, C. *Abilities of man.* New York: Macmillan, 1927.

Stumpf, C. Erscheinungen and psychische Funktionen. *Abbl. preuss. Akad. Wiss.,* Berlin, 1906.

Tenopyr, M. L., Guilford, J. P., & Hoepfner, R. A factor analysis of symbolic-memory abilities. *Reports from the Psychological Laboratory,* no. 38. Los Angeles, Calif.: University of Southern California, 1966.

Thorndike, E. L. Intelligence and its uses. *Harper's Magazine,* 1920, 140, 227-235.

Thurstone, L. L. *Vectors of mind.* Chicago: University of Chicago Press, 1935.

Titchener, E. B. *Experimental study of the thought processes.* New York: Macmillan, 1909.

Titchener, E. B. *Systematic psychology: Prolegomena.* New York: Macmillan, 1929.

Tolman, E. C. *Purposive behavior in animals and man.* New York: Appleton-Century-Crofts, 1932.

Tolman, E. C. There is more than one kind of learning. *Psychological Review,* 1949, 56, 144-156.

Torrance, E. P. *Constructive behavior: Stress, personality, and mental health.* Belmont, Calif.: Wadsworth, 1965.

Vernon, P. E. *The structure of abilities.* New York: Wiley, 1950.

von Neuman, J., & Morgenstern, O. *Theory of games and economic behavior.* Princeton, NJ.: University of Princeton Press, 1944.

Wachtel, P. L. Field differentiation and psychological differentiation: Reexamination. *Perceptual and Motor Skills,* 1972, 35, 179-189.

Wallas, G. *The art of thought.* London: Watts, 1945.

Watson, J. B. *Psychology from the standpoint of a behaviorist,* 2nd ed. Philadelphia: Lippincott, 1929.

Welford, A.T. & Birren, J.E. (eds.), Decision making and age: *Interdisciplinary topics in gerontology, Vol. 4.* Basel: Karger, 1969. Pp. 82-102.

Wertheimer, M. *Productive thinking.* New York: Harper, 1945.

Wiig, E. H., & Semel, E. M. *Language disabilities in children and adolescents.* Columbus, Ohio: Merrill, 1976.

Wilson, R. C., Guilford, J. P., Christensen, P. R., & Lewis, D. J. A factor-analytic study of creative-thinking abilities. *Psychometrika,* 1954, 19, 297-311.

Witkin, H. A. Cognitive styles in learning and teaching. In S. Messick (ed.), *Individuality in learning.* San Francisco: Jossey-Bass, 1976.

Witkin, H. A., Dyk, R. B., Faterson, H. F., Goodenough, D. R., & Karp, S. A. *Psychological differentiation.* New York: Wiley, 1974.

Woodworth, R.S., & Schlossberg, H. *Experimental psychology.* New York: Holt, 1954.

Wooldridge, D. E. *The machinery of the brain.* New York: McGraw-Hill, 1963.

Zimmerman, W. S. A simple graphic method of orthogonal rotation of axes. *Psychometrika,* 1946, 11, 51-55.

NAME INDEX

A

Abe, C., 68, 159
Ach, N., 38
Allen, M. S., 90, 158
Arib, M. A., x, 158
Aschner, M. J., 153, 158

B

Barnard, C. J., 121, 158
Bartlett, M. S., 72, 158
Berger, R. M., 59, 108, 158
Binet, A., 17
Birren, J. E., 165
Borgatta, E. F., 149, 158
Boring, E. G., 95, 158
Bradley, P. A., 43n, 68n, 90, 162
Brentano, F., xi
Broadbent, D. E., x, 158
Broverman, D. M., 135, 158
Brown, S. W., 87, 159
Burt, C., 3n, 7, 19, 159
Bush, R. R., 51, 159

C

Cattell, R. B., 3n, 159
Chorness, M. H., 107, 159
Christensen, P. R., 58, 59, 100, 101, 102,
    104, 108, 136, 139, 158, 159, 163
Cliff, N., 143, 159
Cline, V. B., 68, 159
Cohen, J., 122, 159
Comrey, A. L., 101, 160
Cronbach, L. J., 159
Crossman, E. R. F. W., 31, 159

D

Darwin, C., xi
Dewey, J., 113, 159
Dunham, J. L., 61n, 159
Dyk, R. B., 135, 165

E

Ebbinghaus, H., 47
Edwards, W., 122, 159
Elshout, J. J., 143, 159
Estes, W. K., 51, 160
Eysenck, H. J., 7, 160
Eysenck, S. B. G., 7, 160

F

Faterson, H. F., 135, 165
Feldman, B., 82, 160
Ferguson, G. A., 57, 91, 160
Fisher, R. A., 122, 160
Fleishman, E. A., 56, 61, 160
Frick, J. W., 58, 100, 104, 139, 160

G

Galanter, E., 51, 56, 163
Garner, W. R., x, 160
Garvin, P. L., xi, 160
Getzels, J. W., 68, 160
Goodenough, D. R., 135, 165
Green, R. F., 101, 149, 160
Grings, W. W., 149, 160
Guthrie, E. R., 50, 51, 162
Guttman, L., 5n, 162

H

Hansel, C. E. M., 122, 159
Helson, H., 43, 144, 162
Hempel, W. E., Jr., 56, 160
Hendricks, M., 45, 162
Hoepfner, R., xii, 26, 35, 43n, 45, 46, 61n,
    68n, 81, 87, 89, 90, 106n, 159, 162
Holley, J. W., 144, 162
Horn, J. L., 142-143, 162
Hull, C. L., ix, xi, 49, 54, 162
Hunt, E. B., x, 162

J

Jackson, P. W., 68, 160
James, W., 32

K

Kamstra, O. W. M., 40, 81n, 162
Kant, E., 41
Karlin, J. E., 84, 163
Karp, S. A., 135, 165
Katzenberger, L., 81, 163
Kettner, N. W., 101, 102, 108, 163
Kluever, R. C., 69, 90, 163
Knapp, J. R., 142-143, 162
Kogan, N., 123, 163
Köhler, W., 43, 54, 163
Külpe, O., 95

L

Lacey, J. I., 18, 102, 162
Lazersfeld, P. F., 5n, 162, 163
Lewis, D. J., 108, 136, 165
Lorge, I., 146
Luce, R. D., 122, 163

M

Mahoney, M. J., 155, 163
Marbe, K., 38
Meeker, M. N., 92, 163
Merrifield, P. R., 58, 90, 100, 101, 139,
    158, 163
Messer, A., 38
Messick, S., 139, 140, 141, 163
Miller, G. A., 51, 56, 163
Mosteller, F., 51, 159
Mowrer, O. H., 50, 163

N

Neisser, U., x, 163

Newel, A., x, 164
Nowlis, H. H., 149, 164
Nowlis, V., 149, 164

O

Osgood, C. E., 149, 150, 164

P

Pavlov, I., 50
Piaget, J., 57
Pribram, K. H., 51, 56, 163

R

Riaffa, H., 122, 163
Richards, J. M., Jr. 68, 159
Rossman, J., 114, 164
Royce, J. R., 30, 151, 164
Ryan, T. A., 149, 164

S

Santostefano, S., 135, 164
Schlossberg, H., 56, 150
Scott, W. A., 136, 164
Sells, S. B., 151, 164
Semel, E. M., 151, 165
Shaw, J. C., x, 164
Simon, H. A., x, 121, 164
Skinner, B. F., 49, 164
Spearman, C., 17, 19, 100, 164
Stumpf, C., 40
Suci, G. J., 149, 150, 165

T

Tannenbaum, P. H., 149, 150, 165
Tenopyr, M. L., 87, 164
Thorndike, E. L., 22, 47, 49, 54, 164
Thorndike, R. L., 146
Thurstone, L. L., 17, 18, 164
Titchener, E. B., xi, 37-38, 95, 164, 165
Tolman, E. C., 3n, 51, 165
Torrance, E. P., 155, 165

V

Van Hemert, M., 143, 165
Van Hemert, N. A., 143, 165

W

Wachtel, P. L., 135, 165

Wallach, M. A., 123, 163
Wallas, G., 113-114, 165
Watson, J., ix, 95
Wechsler, D., 146
Welford, A. T., 165
Wertheimer, M., 43, 165
Wiig, E. H., 151, 165
Wilson, R. C., 108, 136, 165
Witkin, H. A., 135, 165
Woodworth, R. S., 56, 150, 165
Wooldridge, D. E., 144, 165

Wundt, W., xi, 36-37, 95, 149, 165

V

Vernon, P. E., 7, 19, 165

Z

Zimmerman, W. S., 104, 142, 165

SUBJECT INDEX

A

Act psychology, 40
Age, and SI abilities, 126-131
Analytical-versus-global style, 138
Arithmetical reasoning, SI functions in, 102-104
Association, and Gestalt psychology, 143
  as implication, 35
  in SI terms, 52
Autonomic functioning, 149

B

Behavior, model for, 31-34
Behaviorism, ix, 41
Brain, and computer, x-xi
  as logical device, 143-144
  and mathematics, 144

C

Cognition, and action, 55-56
  and age, 126-127
  in problem solving, 114
Cognitive controls, education for, 154
Cognitive psychology, defined, x
Cognitive styles, and abilities, 134, 141
  and SI categories, 141
  varieties of, 134, 141
Complexity-versus-simplicity style, 136-137
Computer, and brain, x-xi
Computer simulation, evaluation of, x-xi
Concept, defined, 61
Concept learning, and abilities, 63-67

and cognition, 64
and divergent production, 66-67
and memory, 64-66
Concepts, roles of, in science, 96
  in SI terms, 99
Consciousness, evaluation of, ix
Content psychologies, 36-39
Contiguity, and learning, 50-51
Convergent production, and age, 128-129

Creative thinking, and problem solving, 58-59
  in SI terms, 25, 107-108
  steps in, 113-114
Creativity, defined, 112
  and intelligence, 111-113
Cybernetic function, 31
Cybernetics, and reinforcement, 54

D

Decision making, and administration, 121-122
  and age, 125-131
  in economics, 121
  intelligence and, 123-125
  and problem solving, 124-125
  in statistics, 122
  variables in, 123
  varieties of, 120-121
Deduction, in SI terms, 99-100
Divergent production, and age, 127-128
  preference for, 139

E

Education, imbalances in, 153-154

for intelligence, 57-58
SI in, 153-154
Emotion, dimensions of, 149-150
Emotions, as information, 45
Emotional expressions, analysis of, 27-29
Equivalence-range style, 137
Evaluation, and age, 129
in behavior, 31
in problem solving, 116
and reinforcement, 54-55, 148
Executive functions, 45
analysis of, 26-29
intellectual, 134-135
nature of, 29-30

F

Factor analysis, experimental, 11-13
and psychological theory, 3-5
as scientific method, 10-13, 97-98
statistical tests in, 12
Factor models, dimensional, 5-7
hierarchical, 7-9
matrix, 9-10
Factors, and functions, 13-14
of intelligence, development of, 57-58
in school learning, 73-75
Faculty psychology, 39-40
Feelings, as information, 45
taxonomy of, 149
Field independence versus field dependence, 135-136
Flexibility, adaptive, 101
in problem solving, 118
in SI terms, 100-101
spontaneous, 100
Focusing-versus-scanning style, 138
Formal discipline, 59
Frame of reference, needs for, xi-xii
Functional fixedness, in SI terms, 101
Functional psychology, 40

G

g, Spearman's, 17,19
G index of agreement, 144
Galvanic skin response, 149
Game theory, 122
Gestalt psychology, 41-46, 146
Gottschaldt figures, 135
Group factors, 17

H

Higher Mental Process, 93-94

I

Imageless-thought psychology, 38-39
Implications, and associations, 52
defined, 23
Individual   differences,   approach
through, 13-14, 98-99
in psychological theory, 5
Induction, in SI terms, 99
Information, and age, 130-131
categories of, defined, x, 22-23
evaluation of, ix
Informational psychology, 52
Insight, explained, 53-54
Intellectual-preference styles, 138-139
Intelligence, defined, xi, 89, 112
Intelligence tests, imbalances in, 154
IQ, and creativity, 111-112
tests of, 16-17
Isomorphism, in behavior, 45

K

Kinesthetic information, 30

L

Learning, of concepts, 61-69
defined, 68
in education, 152-153
measurement of, 69-70
repetition and, 91
SI abilities and, 63-67, 73-75
transformations in, 68-75
Leveling-versus-sharpening style, 137
Logical memory, 88-89

M

Mathematics, and the brain, 144
Matrix model, for intelligence, 19-24
for memory, 77
Meaning, context theory of, 37
of words, 149
Meaningful memory, 88
Memory, abilities of, 77-78
and age, 127
for classes, 82-83
definition of, 47-48
experimental controls for, 90
for implications, 87-88
informational varieties of, 90-92
for relations, 83-84
for systems, 84-85
for units, 81-82
for transformations, 85-86
Memory tests, controls in, 79-81

described, 81-88
requirements for, 78-81
Mental health, and SI concepts, 154-155
Moods, factors of, 149-150
and personality traits, 150
Motivation, informational view of, 147-148
phenomena of, 147
Motor activity, SI categories and, 45

N

Numerical-facility factor, 102
Neurology, and SI concepts, 145-146

O

Operational-informational psychology, 24, 36
Operational models, need for, 144-146
Operations, and Learning, 54-55

P

Personality traits, and moods, 150
and cognitive styles, 140
Planning, in SI terms, 108-109
Problem solving, and creative thinking, 58-59
research on, 107
and SI functions, 102-107
SIPS model for, 114-117
steps in, 113-114
Problems, sensitivity to, 109
Products, in Gestalt psychology, 42-43
in learning, 53-54
in motor activity, 30
Product psychologies, 41
Products, roles of in problem solving, 117-119
Psychoanalytic psychology, 39
Psycho-epistemology, 24
Psycho-logic, 24, 144
Psychological test, history of, 38-39
Psychomotor, abilities, 32

R

Reading comprehension, 69-70

Reading disability, 69
Reasoning, in SI terms, 101
Recall versus recognition, in tests, 81
Recall tests, 79-80
Reinforcement, and evaluation, 54-55
Relations, and associations, 52
Risk, in decision making, 123-124

S

Shortcircuiting in behavior, 32
SI model, diagram for, 21
Similarity, judgments of, 137
SIPS model, 115
Speech, SI functions in, 151-152
Stress, and mental health, 155
and SI functions, 155
Structure of intellect, defense of, 142-143
explained, 19-23
implications of, 23-24, 143-144
model for, 22
Systems, and age, 130
and learning, 53
versus relations, 146-147

T

Taxonomic problems, 155-156
Taxonomy, value of, xi
Thinking, concepts for, 95-109
Traits, and functions, 14
Transfer effects, and age, 91
in learning, 56-58
Transformation abilities, described, 70-71
Transformations, defined, 23
and Field Independence, 136
in Gestalt psychology, 43
and learning, 69-75
in school learning, 69

V

Verbal versus nonverbal memory, 89

W

Würzburg psychology, 38